Percy Hetherington Fitzgerald

The Art of Acting

Percy Hetherington Fitzgerald

The Art of Acting

ISBN/EAN: 9783744769341

Printed in Europe, USA, Canada, Australia, Japan

Cover: Foto ©Lupo / pixelio.de

More available books at **www.hansebooks.com**

THE ART OF ACTING.

a

The Dilettante Library.

Frederic Lemaitre.

THE ART OF ACTING

IN CONNECTION WITH THE

STUDY OF CHARACTER, THE SPIRIT OF COMEDY
AND STAGE ILLUSION

BY

PERCY FITZGERALD, M.A, F.S.A.

WITH A PORTRAIT OF FREDERIC LEMAITRE

LONDON
SWAN SONNENSCHEIN & CO.
NEW YORK: MACMILLAN & CO.
1892

MI
r.

Printed by Cowan & Co., Limited, Perth.

NOTE.

The substance of the following little Treatise was delivered in the form of Lectures at the Royal Institution, the Society of Arts, and the Royal Institute, Hull.

INSCRIBED

. TO

MRS. KENDALL.

ABSTRACT OF CONTENTS.

——:o:——

CONTENTS.

CONTENTS.

THE ART OF ACTING.

One of the most engaging and fascinating of the arts, and which has an attraction for those even who do not frequent the theatres, is surely the Art of Acting. This art we must distinguish from the ordinary, rough-and-ready, journeyman sort of performance which is found at many theatres, in which there is little pretence at art; though the system is fairly sufficient, and found satisfactory by audiences. It is no libel on the profession to say that

A

their efforts are not scientific; they
mostly work by an intelligent instinct, or
seem to be directed by "rule of
thumb" principles.   Indeed, we might
say that there are *actors*, and that there
are *performers*.   This distinguishes the
cultured from the uncultured "acting of
commerce."   The question of Dramatic
Schools has often been discussed : it is a
large one; but it can be shown that there
is but the one school for acting—the study
of character; and character is only to be
studied in the great plays and great
comedies, which offer all the turns and
humours of character, and compel the
actor to discover means and devices for
representing them.   Of course, schools
for teaching the drill and *technique* merely,

are most desirable; but that is another thing altogether.

And this Art of Acting,—what an elegant, many-sided art it is! When we find an actor before us equipped with all its resources, graces, and refinements, what form of enjoyment can be so exquisite! Nothing approaches it. But then what a vast number of qualifications are requisite: correct elocution and pronunciation; regulation and command of the voice; melodious cadence, so as to give pleasure to the ear; expression of the face; expression of the eye and mouth; contending emotions, expressed at the same moment or in succession; gesture; dignified walk; the art of wearing clothes; movements suspended with a sort of surprise, and movements that anticipate the expressed meaning.

Tone and " Distinction."

Some of the more elegant and attractive of histrionic gifts are so delicate as to be almost impalpable. They can be felt or inspired, but scarcely can be taught. There is *Tone*, for instance. It is possible to convey the idea of the character without uttering a word or making a move-ment, and simply by tone or colouring. This is a precious and a mysterious gift, and rarely found. We see something akin to it in daily life, when we say that there is " something interesting " in such a person, something attractive, though the

person has scarcely spoken, or moved. This
tone may be acquired by the performer—
by becoming thoroughly permeated with the
essentials of his character, and not by
accidents. Mr. Irving has this gift when ×
playing characters such as *Mathias.* We
find a good deal of this charm in the
works of the Impressionalists, and of Corot,
the French painter. Their principle is to
record the tone of a scene, not the details ; for they tell us that details are not
noticed under such conditions. Thus we
see, of an evening, an inexpressibly melan-
choly tone come over the landscape—like
gloom over the human face : it absorbs
everything into itself—the trees, leaves,
grass, all which these painters present in a
misty way. The outlines of trees, leaves,

branches, all become indistinct masses.
There has been much extravagance in
developing this system, but there can be
little doubt that in the main it is the
basis of art. It opens, too, an interesting
speculation, closely connected too with
histrionic art as to what should be the
limit in presenting details, and at what
point we should stop.

Connected with this is another great gift
—that of *Distinction*—also an impalpable
quality, and little known in the profession.
It is unintelligible to your journeyman
actor. We hear of an "actor of distinction," or that he imparted "distinction" to
the character; it is felt, but difficult to
define. Distinction seems to be a disdain of
vulgar details, of all trivial means and pro-

cesses. The actor despises or ignores trifles. In real life a commonplace person, who is the opposite of a person with " distinction," is abundant in details, and very voluble in words, and explanations, and gestures, which to him · are all-important. He thinks accidents and trivialities of moment; whereas one with the gift of distinction conceives everything in a large spirit, and sees the essence of things. He, in short, expresses himself by the agency of mind rather than by any mechanical means. It is almost impossible to analyse this special charm ; it comes, of course, from a native grace of soul, refinement, and elegance, and an absence of affectation—which quality, in a performer, is vulgarity. Difficult to define, it seems the result of high culture and practice.

It suggests something of the effect produced
when a well-bred man of the world enters a
room, who, though he says or does nothing,
impresses. One man has an air of reserve,
though he may not be given to silence; another has force of character; a third is poetical of aspect. There is something of this in
what is said of a well-dressed man: that
you do not see or know *how* he is dressed.
One of our most celebrated portrait painters,
who is remarkable for his brilliant colouring,
his vigorous handling and good likenesses,
seems always to fail in this matter of distinction. He lacks it because he *rests* in his
methods, not in the spiritual element.
Whatever objection may be taken to Mr.
Irving's acting and style, his greatest op-
ponents must admit that in whatever he

does, whether in mounting a play, or in standing on the stage, or moving across the scene, there is always this "note" of "distinction." He is apart from his fellows. To him, on his own stage at the Lyceum, seem specially to apply the words of Shakespeare,

> " As in a theatre, the eyes of men,
> After a well-grac'd actor leaves the stage,
> Are idly bent on him that enters next.'

Exquisitely dramatic lines that seem charged with the flutter and excitement of the moment. It is just after some intense or thrilling incident; the well-grac'd actor has gone: there is an air of vacancy. Our eyes, idly bent on the rest, have followed him—his tones still ring in our ears. The others are left; but they seem creatures earthy as ourselves; *they* have not "distinction." This contrast is often extraordinary; and there are players who contrive to vulgarise, instead of "distinguishing," everything they touch.

Breadth.

"Breadth" is another of the mysterious powers which come from within, and is the result of intellectual force. It arises from the actor being able to *enrich* a simple sentence, or even a word, with its fullest meaning, with all the associations and illustrations of which it is capable. The old, experienced actor, well trained in the provinces and in all the old pieces, has "breadth." Seeing one of these veterans in a modern company, we are struck by the contrast he offers to his other companions. All he says has *breadth;* whereas in their utterances there is a thinness and leanness, even though they strive and do their best to supply breadth by *extra* emphasis, and the raising of their voice. And how have these old actors acquired *breadth?* Simply by acting in the old pieces which *have* breadth, and are so stored with thoughts and suggestions, that when they come to utter a sentence, the rich stock of ideas rushes on them, and forces them to give them some intelligent shape and utterance. This might be made clearer by a familiar illustration. A young man is asked by his old uncle to dine, and he will say "yes" coldly enough. But were he asked unexpectedly by the father of the young lady to whom he is attached and who is opposed to his pretensions, we would venture to say, were we listening, that we would recognise in that simple "yes," a whole tide of different emotions. There would be *joy, eagerness, love, gratitude, hope, flutter,* and the rest—yet all conveyed in that little monosyllable "yes."

There is a scene in our old, antiquated friend, "The Hunchback," where Julia has just dismissed her lover, Sir Thomas Clifford. Helen, her friend and confidante, is congratulating her, and ridicules and gibes at the discarded admirer, when Julia says, "I hate you, *Helen.*" Lately a very capable actress was performing the part, and she gave these three little, but significant, words in an easy, comfortable,

sort of way, according to its simple meaning, "I hate you, *Helen.*" Yet this was once
one of the grand points of the play, and
used to "bring down the house." It was
really a whole situation. *Julia* still loved
Clifford, but pride was at work on both
sides. She was vexed with *herself;* she
felt that she ought to do as *Helen* advised ;
that she did not hate her at all, but herself. So, it should be spoken in a tone of
grief and irresolution—" I—I—I *hate* you,
Helen ! "

Again: Munden, a famous comic actor at
the beginning of the century, at the close
of a scene, sees a jug of beer on a table,
and says merely, "Some gentleman has left
his beer." On the modern stage, a comic
actor would probably wink slyly at the

audience, and, seizing the beer, drink it off. Munden made a whole scene out of this— first repeating the words in a ruminative way, as if it were an indifferent piece of news; then in a tone of enjoyment; then in a suspicious tone, as though he were being watched.   Every moment he was drawing nearer.   In short, it was a picture in little of a temptation, and gradual fall; and all arising out of a quart pot.

There is an account (in the "New Monthly" Magazine of 1829) of a French actress, Mademoiselle Vertprè, which happily illustrates the charm of these nameless delicacies. " A 'oui' or 'non' from her lips is eloquent music, even when it has no particular meaning; but when it has a particularly pointed or condensed meaning, its effect is more potent than a whole speech. Nay, there is no moment when, though she says nothing, she is not speaking—either by a dead, statue-like stillness or a hardly imperceptible movement, advancing! or retreating of her delicate body, or an indescribable and nameless motion of one or both the shoulders, too gentle to be called a jerk, and too graceful for a shrug—or, finally, that ineffable little female toss of the head, the effect of which it is as impossible to escape as to either describe, or account for." Then there was " the intensely feminine air which pervades everything she . does—seeming to arise from an ever present, and ever active feeling of sex—you never for an instant lose sight of the woman in the character: one of the great secrets of attaining and preserving that personal ascendency over the audience which none but women ever possess, and which even they cannot maintain in connection with any very striking representation of particular characters." How true is this! Many of our actresses lose sight of their sex and its graces: they become cold, hard, noisy, and harsh of voice, in obedience to the necessities of the scene, and from their efforts to give "point" to what they say and do. All delicacies are thus lost: they seem to be contending with the men, and on the same ground.

Should an Actor Feel?

We now come to a more interesting question—Should an actor really *feel* the

emotions he is depicting? Should he shed
real tears, utter genuine sobs, and would
the performance gain by his so doing?
This point was first started by Diderot, the
French philosopher, over a century ago,
in what is called his " Paradoxe," which was
recently translated by Mr. Walter Pollock,
with an interesting introduction added
by Mr. Irving. It gave rise to much dis-
cussion. Johnson, in his rough way,
declared that an actor who, even for a
moment, could work himself up to feel
like a murderer, ought to be executed after
the play was over. But there can be little
doubt that it must be decided in the nega-
tive; on the ground that such emotional
exhibitions are *undramatic,* and that so
much *realism* is mere crude nature. Indeed,

B

such *naturalism*, or Zolaism, seems out of keeping with the artistic and abstract associations of the stage.

A more serious objection is, that in this state the actor loses control of himself—and the effect accordingly *ceases to be an artistic display*. The actor, instead of controlling, is himself controlled. Were we to push the theory farther, the best way to represent sickness, or a person in a fever, would be to bring forward a really *sick* actor ; or in the case of intoxication, have the actor made intoxicated behind the scenes, and sent on. Yet, as we know, such realism would add nothing to the dramatic interest. And further, there is the serious objection taken by Diderot himself, that after several nights the fountain of tears would dry up, and, with our runs of from 100 to 200 nights, Niobe herself would be found unequal to the supply.

"To keep one's head," said Regnier, "while appearing to give up one's heart, is the secret." Mr. R. Solly quotes Guizot: " To successfully depict a passion, it is certainly necessary to be capable of feeling it, sometimes to have experienced it : but to feel it at the moment is not necessary, and often does harm rather than good." Talma and Coquelin also hold the same view. Diderot goes so far as to maintain that "in the complete absence of sensibility is the possibility of a fine actor," and then describes him as watching himself, listening to the tones of his own voice to see if it be equal to his standard In other words he

" gives us the recollections of his emotions."
This seems to go too far.   I am convinced,
as Mr. Irving explained it recently, in his
lecture before an Edinburgh meeting, that
"the true method, or compromise; is that
the actor must have some emotion, or tendency to emotion, but he must keep it in
hand," and watchfully regulate its course.
Were only the phenomena of emotion exhibited, the audience would not be touched.

Facial Expression.

Now, if the average actor has a fixed
principle, it is that there is but one effective
method of expressing himself—and that is,
by tongue, or speech.   This is his end-all
and be-all.   Should he wish to be angry or

excited, he raises his voice; to be hateful
or jealous, he lowers it; and so on. But
there is a means of expression far more
potent, far more swift, direct, and instan-
taneous, and which in a flash will express
what it would take minutes to utter—that
is THE FACE. Facial expression is wonderful
for all that it conveys, and for the immense
force with which it conveys it. We have
only to think of its multiplied resources—
the power of the eye and the eyebrows, the
mouth, the nostrils. In foreign theatres,
facial expression is a regular part of stage
education, and there is a regular system.
It is so delicate an instrument, that it
conveys the expression, in advance as it
were. In real life we all speak with our
faces, and read each other's faces in antici-

pation. We note the pleasure, or dis-
pleasure, or pain, before a word is spoken.
A wonderful art this when we think of it—
to express the mind in the face. And what a
multiplied power of expression is there in it :
the power of the eye, of the eyebrows, the
mouth, the nostrils even—all which can be
used in combination. But it is a delicate,
sensitive instrument. We feel an emotion ;
it rushes *instantly* to the face and reveals itself. In conversation half the work is done
by the face : we read each other's faces, we
anticipate the coming utterance. It is, in
fact, the *shorthand* of talk—and we have
only to imagine conversation carried on
in darkness, to see how halting and imperfect it would be. It is comparatively
neglected on our stage, but foreign actors

do marvels with their faces. It is a wonderful art, when we think of it—thus to *force*
the mind upward into the face.

And here is the wondrous value of facial
expression for the actor, and for dramatic
purposes generally, *viz.* the magical, and
electrical influence it exercises on the be-
holders. Any *display* of contending emotions
in the face holds us enthralled like a little
drama. How interesting, for instance, to
see some young girl, unsophisticated, fresh
from the country, a little confused at her
novel situation, over whose face the by-
standers see flitting and chasing each other
all sorts of emotion : first shyness, then
eagerness, then distress at having revealed
her thoughts ; while we notice that, all the
time, the spectators have their eyes riveted

on her face ; they follow these changes with smiling and sympathising glances, and attend to little else. Is not this a lesson for our actor? as it surely supplies him with a cheap and ready method of holding his audience in the exactly same fashion.

It should be borne in mind that facial expression is the expression of things that *cannot be spoken*—it is a new language, where language. fails. The contention of great passions can be efficiently expressed only by the face ; you may, of course, describe them in words, but that does not *exhibit* them. A dishonest servant is detected ; you see in his face, firstly, shame, then rage, dislike, defiance, cringing, terror, indecision ; the whole story is to be read there. Another complex expression is the being

" amused." Something is being told with the purpose of deceiving, or impressing the listener ; but he is shrewd enough to understand the true state of the case. And his face shows that he does ; he cannot help being entertained by this contrast ; though he, at the same time, by his words and bearing, appears to accept the narrative. Thus is there a double manifestation—belief on the surface, disbelief within. This, it may be conceived, is a very delicate operation, nay, of the highest delicacy. Even the would-be deceiver feels somehow that he is not being credited, though he has to accept the assurances.

It constantly happens, says Mr. Raymond Solly, in his lately issued, interesting little tract on acting, that, before beginning to speak, some feeling or idea should be indicated, in advance, as it were, of the first words spoken. This sort of reservation is implied in the little words, "but," "however," "nevertheless," etc.; and conveys that there has been a little debate going on within—a hesitation—a conflict of motives. This should be shown in the look or bearing, and the listener is, as it were, taken into confidence. Without this due emphasis, the "but" being glibly uttered without pause, the dramatic significance is lost, and it is actually conveyed that there has been no doubt or hesitation whatever. Got, a great histrionic instructor, always impressed on his pupils this art of suggesting deliberation. Whenever there is a change of idea or new departure, it should be heralded by an anticipating glance or movement. "An actor should always appear to think, not to know."

"The actor," Talma tells us, " must learn the art of thinking before he speaks; and, by introducing pauses, he appears to meditate upon what he is about to say. But his physiognomy must correspond with the suspension of his voice. His attitude and features must indicate that during these moments of silence his soul is deeply engaged; without this his pauses will seem rather to be the result of defective memory, than a secret of his art."

I can now fancy our actor protesting that all this is Utopian: and that no face, on or off the stage, can be made to perform such feats and prodigies. But we have only to visit the remarkable Gallery of the Garrick Club, and gaze at the wonderful portraits displayed on its walls : and these prove what can be done in this way. The faces are literally brimming over with expression; they are gnarled, and scored, and delved with deep lines of drollery or humour. The emotions within seemed to have forced their way to the face, and left their mark, just as suffering does. No wonder the old Macklin declared that he had not lines, but cordage in his face : and it was said of Garrick, that no man's face "showed more wear and tear"—owing to the constant expression of marked emotions.

But in his own vivid way Charles Lamb shows what could be done by the face in these old days, and by one of these old actors. He is speaking of Dodd, one of the good low comedians: "In expressing slowness of apprehension, this actor surpassed all others. You could see the first dawn of an idea stealing slowly over his countenance, climbing up by little and little, with a painful process, till it cleared up at last to the fulness of a twilight conception—its highest meridian. He seemed to keep back his intellect, as some have had the power to retard their pulsation. The balloon takes less time in filling than it took to cover the expansion of his broad moony face over all its quarters with expression. A glimmer of understanding would appear in a corner of his eye, and for lack of fuel go out again. A part of his forehead would catch a little intelligence, and be a long time in com-

municating it to the remainder." Such an
exhibition seems to us lost art, and, it may
be doubted if it could be attempted by any
performer of our day.[1]

Innumerable indeed are the arts and devices which belong to real acting. Acting, in
fact, should go on during every moment that
the player is upon the stage. It has been,
happily, said, "that there is nothing so difficult as to do nothing on the stage, when the
part requires you to do nothing." For

---

[1] The faces of most great actors are remarkable in
this way: notably those of Garrick, Kemble, Kean,
Cooke, Macklin, Phelps, Irving and others. Meeting
any of these in the street, we must turn to look after
them. The French faces, more mobile, and more exercised, are still more striking. I have a collection of
photographs of leading comedians and *farçeurs*, which
are truly astonishing. The most extraordinary is that
of Frederic Lemaitre, which is the frontispiece of this
little book.

this "doing nothing" is acting. More essential still is the acting to another's acting: that is, the helping to act *his* part. This is not much attended to on our stage, or is carried out in an artificial way: the player transparently compelling himself to attend to his companion. There can be even an air of inattention, with an occasional rousing of the attention, as though obliged to attend, and this attracts the audience. " I know," said Dickens' friend, Regnier, " how difficult it is to listen, more difficult even than to speak. Help your comrades! " Nothing so facilitates the task of another actor as this real sympathetic attention. Nay, it will prompt him to new efforts, new and more natural tones and emphasis. " It is essential," goes on Regnier, " that there should be a close connection between all the actors in the same scene." It is equally certain, too, that the absence of such attention will injure the other's efforts. " If you allow your look," says Coquelin, " to become inexpressive, your eyes to wander or exhibit any lack of interest, the public is at fault." It also loses its interest.

Our modern stage system, however, is opposed to the exhibition of facial expression. There is such a flood of light, and the face is so bathed in effulgence, from above and below, that there is little relief. There are no shadows. The eye is distracted by the general garishness. As it is said, " you cannot see the wood for the trees," so here you cannot see the face for the light. Now, under the old dispensation, there was a better system : the light was furnished by four chandeliers, which hung over the actors' faces; the rest of the stage was in comparative shadow mystery, and the figures and faces stood out with a sort of brilliancy. Thus it will be seen how the eye was concentrated on the central objects, because it had nothing else to attract or distract it.

It is odd, however, that, instead of this facial expression, we should have a strange substitute in what is called "the make-up." There is actually an art of make-up, and some actors—performers, shall we say?— have achieved quite a reputation for this spurious device. They contrive to give themselves an altogether new face and figure ; so that friends in front do not recognise

c

them for some moments. We have actually in these days false noses worn in serious characters, which formerly were confined to pantomimes and burlesques. This seems rather ignoble work. But there is a curious Nemesis to come: for the actors who lean on these methods will find their intellectual powers dwindle, and grow more and more enfeebled. It is like swimming with bladders.

There is a passage in Bishop Butler's famous " Analogy " which proves this very effectively—though it may seem a little incongruous introducing a grave and reverend prelate in this connection. He is speaking of what he calls passive and active emotions; and he shows that indulgence in the one exclusively, becomes destructive of the other. Thus, there is pity or compassion felt at the sight of a distressful object: that is the *passive* emotion: the relieving of it, the active principle. Now, if a person indulges in the mere sentiment without following it up, he will find his active charity gradually disappear; and thus we see sentimental people, who *weep over novels*, and are greatly affected by sad sights, are quite unpractical; they do not give anything. On the other hand, persons of active charity—doctors, nurses, and sisters of charity—lose sentiment altogether, and appear unfeeling. This may seem rather metaphysical; but it will be easy to apply it to this "make-up" system, which represents the passive principle. The performer finds himself perpetually devising

fresh "makes up," with a recurring difficulty of contriving novelty. The more it
is indulged in, the more it will destroy
the intellectual or active principle. On
the other hand, the intellectual actor,
who disdains these arts, will find a substitute for them, and can assume what
aspect he wishes. Thus he will have an intellectual "make-up," coming from within.
It was often told of Lablache that he
could actually represent a thunderstorm
by his face, the gathering clouds, the
storm breaking and clearing off, etc. : that
is, he did not imitate it—but he *suggested*
it, which is the true principle.

Elocution.

I think it will be generally admitted

that there is little attempt at formal *elocution* on our stage. Every one says his say, as best he can, and in his own way. And curiously enough this neglect appears to be of a set purpose, and carried out with intention, and for the simple reason that it is not wanted. For the standard of imitation is nothing but the familiar colloquial tone of talk adopted outside, in the streets and houses. But as we know, from painful experience, this is a very disagreeable and earthy form of speech. These rude, sloppy, careless utterances of common conversation may serve for every-day life, but are unsuited to the stage or its dignity. Often we cannot hear even a portion of what is said; the words seem to be dropped, or swallowed. This sort of unfinished speech leaves on us an impression of meanness, and gives the idea that the sentiment, which comes to us in this vulgar guise, must be mean and vulgar also. The key or pitch should be loftier than that of ordinary life, because everything on the stage is an exaggeration. This can be well understood. From lack of training, the actor is uncertain as to the pitch or key of his organ; he has not learned to speak in the low tone, without effort, which shall be sufficient. Passages which should be given with an easy spontaneousness, are uttered with a loud, emphatic and forced declamation; in fact, the general key is noisy and artificial, suggesting recitation. This unnatural key is owing to lack of command over the organ, and the actor is compelled to raise his voice, as being the only way he knows of making himself heard. What a treat to hear " Le Misanthrope " at the Français, given in these elegant, harmonious cadences, when we feel that it is exactly in keeping with the rich laced dresses, the flowing wigs, as well as with the antique and somewhat pedantic sentiments.

Nobody has suffered so much from this blemish as Shakespeare. Even in the best and most conscientious revivals we find an attempt to bring him down to the colloquial measures of the day. We hear the young Venetian nobles rattling over their melodious and poetical lines in the tone of young " mashers." There is no time given for the audience to grasp the meaning. It becomes a sort of gabble. And there is always the glaring contrast between the high and noble thoughts, and exquisite poetical conceits, and the frivolous, idle tone in which they are delivered.

There are some traditional blemishes which, strange to say, are clung to on our stage. Such, for instance, is the lack of " spontaneousness." With new performers, everything is *recited*, even ostentatiously, with the air of having been got by heart. There is no hesitation. And when two persons are carrying on a conversation, the speeches are made with promptness and rapidity, without a moment's pause for thought. The French excel in this air of spontaneousness. They seem to say everything as if it had

just then *occurred to them* at the moment;
nay, there is a sort *of hesitation*, as if they
were looking for the idea or the word : the
thing comes out in the most natural way.
Another strange anomaly is, that in critical
situations, instead of showing hurry and
agitation, our players become solemnly slow
and measured—even at the most agonis-
ing moment. When the hero is about to
destroy himself, or to be killed, or when
the enemy is bursting in the doors, he begins to utter his sentences with a solemn,
and extra slow, deliberation. All this is
out of nature; for a person thus agitated
feels that there is not an instant to be lost;
he hurries to and fro ; he crowds his words
together. So when reproaches are uttered
on some desertion, faithlessness, or betrayal,

the words pour out with extraordinary rapidity, jostling each other at the door of the lips, as it were. This is a common, regular form on the French stage.

Again, take the method of delivering an " aside." These are *spoken trumpet-tongued*, and often at good length, while the other performers suspend operations until the speech is quite finished. Often actors run into the other extreme, and give " hoarse whispers," in which process the voice is forced or pumped out in an extraordinary, unnatural manner, as unlike a real whisper as could be conceived. So with laughter. The regular " stage laugh " is really like nothing in life. Instead of being involuntary, it is purposed and *voluntary*, projected forth in a series of " Ha !

ha! ha's!" Now most persons laugh
silently—indeed, the laugh is seen more
than it is heard. It is a series o " rippling"
smiles or "chuckles;" but the laugh of
enjoyment is mostly internal. Nor do we
often see what may be called the *nuances* of
laughter—that is, the incipient smiling—
the attempt at enforced gravity—the sudden,
overpowering burst—the struggle between
gravity and jest.

Then there is another view. Every
play has, or should have, a particular tone
or key. The claims of actors, the pro-
minence of particular incidents, all should
be subsidiary to this. This tone is even
more important in setting forth the play
itself—in giving what is the true note
or key of the whole. Mr. Irving attends

particularly to this matter — he brings all into harmony, softening down some portions, and setting others in proper relief, like the conductor of an orchestra. But the common practice is, that every one is given license to make the most of his own character, without regard to the interests of the piece. This system is adopted in dealing with revived, old-fashioned plays, and presents them before us very unfairly. Their strained sentiment often causes hilarity, and is condemned as inherently "out of date," absurd, and "exploded." But had the actors transported themselves back to the period and tried to realise the feeling and conditions, under which the piece had been first presented, the effect would be very different. Indeed, the method used is to give it a modern air—to slur over the old-fashioned sentiment; and, by a sort of colloquial, familiar tone, force it to take the shape of every-day life.[1]

The result is a lack of proportion—an exaggeration of unimportant matters —which has the result of enfeebling the really significant portions of the play. I remember, on the production of a truly pastoral drama—which is founded on the simple habits and super-

[1] For instance, there is the familiar " Praise from Sir Hubert Stanley is praise indeed," always greeted with merriment, and the reason is that the actor has *no* faith in the sincerity of the speech, and does not believe in it. But we could quite conceive some one saying, in the House of Commons, that praise from some reserved, sarcastic member "would be praise indeed," and there would be no laugh.

stitions of the peasants of the South of France—" L'Arlésienne," not an opera, but a serious drama illustrated by Bizet's lovely music, the English actors, knowing nothing of this atmosphere, were directed to "make the most" of their parts, which they did according to their lights. They turned them into English low comedy rustics—matter-of-fact people —and I need not say with the most ludicrous effect. All the tone, the poetry, vanished utterly.

And I may add here that, in the performance of Shakespeare's plays, this want of proportion is too often shown. The manager, who wishes to have a grand spectacular exhibition, when dealing with the incidents, seizes on and develops some trifling incident which Shakespeare only meant to dwell on, *en passant*, as it were. At the beginning of " Romeo and Juliet " there is a conflict between the rival houses. We have seen this actually worked into a grand effect and sensation—the stage filled with angry crowds, pouring in from the side streets; windows thrown open ; alarm bells ringing ; a general battle. But it was really only a street scuffle between a few partisans. So with the wrestling match in " As You Like It," for which the stakes are pitched, a ring formed, and excited crowds gathered round, as though it were a tournament. So with the fencing scene in " Hamlet," often turned into a grand formal " bout," or match, before a full court. It was really only a slight social incident : just as in this modern time, a game at billiards or at lawn tennis, might be suggested at a country house. This idea of spontaneousness and carelessness would make the scene infinitely more natural, and more tragic.

Not long since was revived the old-fashioned, highly-strung, fossilised play of "The Stranger," whose sentiment has always seemed forced and unnatural. All the actors did their best to glide over these passages, and to give them a colloquial, familiar turn ; instead of, as they ought to have done, throwing themselves into their parts with perfect sincerity and faith. A feeling of reality would then have been infused into the

whole. Some years ago, when Mr.
Hollingshead was manager of the Gaiety,
and giving burlesques, there was a clamour
raised for good old sterling comedies, such
as it was said were given in the "palmy"
days of the drama. Growing fatigued at
these complaints, and nettled at the hard
things that were said of his taste, he announced that he would revive what he
called in his bills "palmy day dramas;"
and accordingly we were treated to a series
of such old, meritorious fossils, as "George
Barnwell," "The Castle Spectre," "The
Miller and his Men," and such things.
The result was roars of laughter, and
the ingenious manager was admitted to
have completely proved his case. But
had he? The pieces were performed

D

by burlesque actors as a sort of joke. They did not know how to play them. The old actors had faith in these things. Their audiences were "in touch," as it were. They were performed with infinite care, and even elegance. But it would be "forcing an open door" to dwell further on this point.

Gesture.

Gesture on our stage is, I think, chiefly prompted by the *instinct* of the moment. But abroad, it is quite *scientific*, and elaborated, perhaps after the rules of Lavater and others, with the result of very striking and original effects, which would rather astonish some of our professors. Gesture, regulated and studied, is nearly as potent a medium of expression as the voice itself; in many cases it is more subtle, swift, and comprehensive. There is a language in gesture, with innumerable shades of meaning. It will convey everything—doubt, hesitation, eagerness, anger, joy, sorrow; with many more delicate emotions for which words are too formal, and too slow

There is one method of great force, and which is used to enrich the dramatic expression. It is, indeed, quite a common form on the French boards, but almost unknown to us. This is the anticipation of the utterance by the gesture. As an accomplished actress has truly said, "With us it is more art than nature; with the French it is more nature than art." The

body seems to run eagerly forward, in
advance of the mind, as a sort of *avant
courier*. The dramatic result, which ha
extraordinary effect in the way of riveting
attention, seems to work in this fashion. The
anticipatory gesture is made. Then arise
in the spectator's mind a sort of speculation
as to whether the utterance to follow wil
correspond. Then a second or two o
suspense follows; all is finally satisfied
by the utterance itself. There is a passage
in one of Goldsmith's essays, where he
describes the acting of Clairon, the grea
French actress. " On her first speech," he
says, " her hands and tongue never set ou
together, *but the one prepares us for the
other*. She sometimes begins with a mute
eloquent attitude ; but never goes forward

all at once, with hands, eyes, head, and voice. By this simple beginning is given a power of *rising* in the passion of the scene." This is an invaluable technical lesson for an actor; and what a light it throws, and how scientific is the device!

There are other devices—the suspended or intercepted gesture: (the classical " *quos ego,*") the attempt at self-mastery; and what is more effective than the simple gesture of despair, without a single word being spoken, and which conveys so much? Even where gesture has no particular significance, it is always welcome and agreeable to the eye.[1]

---

[1] Lord Dufferin, in a recent interesting address, recalled one valuable hint that had been given him by a well-known actor, who pointed out to him that

The tendency, therefore, of gesture is in the direction of reserve, and economy of motion. It has been said by a French teacher, "The more we multiply gestures, the more we make them insignificant." Fenelon tells us, "It is not natural to be always using gestures in speaking; one should move the arms because one is animated, but *should not move them in order to appear animated.*" There is a world of suggestion in this. Johnson, having the extravagant gestures of the players of his time before him, declared that, "The action of all the players in tragedy is bad.

there is weakness suggested, when the *palms* of the hand are put forward, as is commonly done. The idea of power and strength was conveyed by turning the backs of the hands to the audience.

It should be a man's study *to repress the signs of emotion* and passion, as they are called "—the repression being even more significant. A French professor, M. Dupont-Vernon, has gone to the root of the matter when he lays it down that gesture is a language to express ideas *that are not written*, that is, those delicate, almost impalpable thoughts and shadows of thoughts, for which words are too coarse and inefficient.

One of our more refined actresses, now unhappily withdrawn from the stage, Miss Anderson, arrayed in her classical or Empire dress, as she moved about or sank into a chair, always gave pleasure from the grace she imparted to the movement. This movement was a language, for it

spoke of refinement and grace, and of a
refined nature within.   It amounted to an
uttered sentence, as though we had heard
something refined, though not taking any
distinct shape.

Even the folds of the drapery multiply
the expression. Thus, the bare arm may be
raised with a graceful movement, and be-
token some refined sentiment.   But place a
drapery on the arm, and each fold will assume an elegant form ; thus we have innumerable shapes of expression instead of
one, because each fold is the result of the
feeling transmitted from within to the arm ;
from the arm to the drapery; and from the
drapery to the folds.   It may even be said
that the wearing of old-fashioned clothes is
an art in itself, some performers carrying

them as if to the manner born, as though they were their habitual garments; while others wear them with an air of stiff discomfort, as if not at ease in them. One of our best actors, Mr. Hare, is so conscientious in this matter, that he always wears his clothes of antique cut in his own house for some days before the performance, so as to feel quite "easy" in them, and thus grow familiar to the constraint. This constraint shows affectation : the mistaking of means for the end ;—the actor is thinking of his clothes rather than of the purpose for which clothes are worn.

"Reserve" is yet another admirable histrionic gift. The actor seems to convey that he has a sort of "storage" of force : that there are powers of speech and action laid up and kept ready. The idea of force unused, but ready, is in itself a force, and there is a sort of mystery attending it. Silence, recollection, even in social life, will thus impress us. Vulgar minds associate power, with its manifestation, either by speech or action. Connected with this is the gift of "propriety," by which we would understand the limits of expression : that is the extent to which an actor should go in exhibiting the phenomena of his character. But too often he will employ every art, every idea that suggests itself, to enhance the effect, without reflecting that enough has been done. Occasionally we see characters performed with an exquisite "propriety." We feel that no touch is wanting, and that not another touch could be added. The effect left is of perfect satisfaction. On the other hand, how commonly do we not feel that a representation is quite unlike what such a situation would be in real life, that a person in ordinary society would be wholly different. We often see such persons acquitting themselves with a becoming tact, and reserve, and acknowledge that they have behaved as the situation required—doing neither more nor less than was necessary. This is "propriety."

"*Stage Business.*"

And now we should consider how great, and excessive even, is the value and importance of movements of all kinds upon the stage, and which are so apt to be considered trivial and of small significance. The stage is, as the name betokens, only a raised platform, the centre to which a thousand pair of eyes are to be directed. And it is odd to think that there is no other situation in life where people exhibit this fixity of gaze, and keep their eyes riveted on an object for hours together. No sermon or religious rite can secure the same absorbing attention. And the result of this conspicuousness is, that to everything that is done on that platform, the spectator *must* attach a meaning and significance, and this though none be intended. It is like a number of men repairing the top of a high steeple, with a crowd in the street

below staring at them : hence every movement made, every little detail of the work, is
watched with the deepest interest. And
this is fully shown by considering what a
play really is. A play, or theatrical story,
is a portion of real life, but highly condensed
and compressed ; so that what would cover
years or months, here takes place in an
hour or two—a conversation that would
fill half-an-hour, here must fill only five
minutes. In space there is the same ab-
breviation. A market-place or square,
or a room in a palace, must here be squeezed
into very few feet. Hence the exaggeration
of what is called the "stage walk," each
step being equivalent to many steps in
significance. Therefore, to be in proportion, sentiments, speeches, movements, every-

thing must be *selected*, as it were, and there must be nothing but what must have a meaning. Thus it is with gesture. And so it is with the "crossings," which we find marked in the prompter's copy; these are usually set down with a view to please the eye—capriciously enough—or to break up the monotony of the action. After a certain length of conversation, one actor is directed to "cross" the other, and he starts afresh. But these "crossings," on the principles we have been considering, should have real significance. They are a method of expression. Suppose a gentleman conversing with a lady in her drawing-room. Were he to rise suddenly, "cross" and sit down on the other side, she would naturally interpret this as agitation, and possibly think that a declaration was going to follow. So with walking, or the "stage stride." In society, no one walks about; or if he did it would be thought to mean something. Everyone's eyes in a drawing-room would follow with astonishment the man who was thus promenading the room. On the stage there is this constant, unmeaning motion; but it would be most useful if it expressed anything.

So important do the French consider any change or movement on the stage, that when a fresh character comes on, or goes off, they call it a *new scene*, as we can see in their play books. Even in the lower limbs,— often the least dignified portion of the figure,—there is a sort of expression. As we are speaking of the figure, I may mention a curious distortion which arises from the situation of the stalls, and which may not have been noticed. Few would imagine that the feet and lower limbs of the performers are some feet nearer to us than their faces. This is reversing the order of things, and destroys scenic illusion. For we are looking at people in the wrong way. In real life we look at them downwards, or on a level. In the face everything is sheltered, and under a sort of penthouse. The hair shelters the forehead—the eyebrows, the eyelids—the eyelids, the eyes—the nose, the mouth—the mouth, the teeth. This half-veiling—such as the hair covering part of the ear—has a sort of dramatic or artistic significance. But when we sit in the stalls, this is reversed. The revelation of the anatomy is disagreeable. We see upwards into the mouth, the palate, look up the nostrils even. The players' faces really seem to us like some sort of marine monsters—dog-fishes and the like. The shadows are all reversed. But when we look from the proper level—from the grand tier, which in the old well-designed theatres is a little above the line of the stage—the illusion is restored. This alone would show that the stalls are about the worst place for scenic illusion.

Lately I was conversing with a veteran play-goer, of immense age, who had known intimately, and seen often, the great John Kemble. He described to me, with rapture almost, his performance of the lugubrious "Stranger"—particularly the meeting with

E

Mrs. Haller; and my venerable friend then sat down in an arm-chair to show me how it was done.   As the erring lady drew near, the great John began to exhibit the strongest agitation, in his knees and legs; as she came nearer they quivered with more and yet more rapidity; and, as the old man assured me, the audience were profoundly affected by this exhibition. This seems rather comical, but still it is high authority.

And now, it will be asked, why are all these true, simple, and very obvious prin- ciples of acting neglected, which are so certain in their results—*so* certain, too, to add to the attractions, popularity, and profits of an actor?   The answer is that another form of entertainment has been

substituted, a sort of rarce-show, or panoramic exhibition—intended for the eye
rather than for the intellect, and whose
attraction, as we have seen, is exhausted by
repetition. And when in some lucid
interval of good sense we are presented
with a bit of acting that is founded on the
old, true principles—its reception is so
eager, and tumultuous, that it becomes an
even more astonishing problem, that such
an entertainment is not supplied. The
reason would seem to be that the spurious
article is cheaper, and can be manufactured
easily and at once. The mere imitative
actor can "get on the stage" without study
or preparation : for what he is set to do
needs scarcely any study or preparation·
Real acting is a science, to be studied and

mastered, as other sciences are studied and mastered, by long years of training.

Realism.

These things—minutely as we have treated them—form but the " drill " and discipline of the stage. They are akin to the arts and methods of the painter, who must learn to "prime" his canvas, what colours to lay on over other colours— how to contrast them and the like ; the mere mechanism of the craft, which it takes years to acquire. But *acting*, and the great science of acting, is still far off. We are only at the threshold, and the person who may have laboriously studied and mastered the principles we have been considering has not as yet begun to *act.* It will be interesting now to discuss this very important question.

First, we must ask ourselves, "What is the foundation of all. dramatic interest? What is it that so enchains our eyes, and ears, and faculties to the stage?" Not surely the shows and panoplies going on; or the elaborate "make-up," however clever: not the exact imitation of peculiarities, voice, action, grotesque motions, the perfect *replica*, in short, of the type— not any of these material things. The real attraction for the audience is the exhibition of *character;* and the accurate presentation of character, with all its contrasts, and mysterious tones, founded on study and observation, is what constitutes *acting.*

There is no intellectual pastime more delightful than the observation of character. As we pass along the streets, or descend to "the underground," or mount to the garden seats on the familiar omnibus—no bad coign of vantage—endless dramas are being played about us; touches of comedy, and humour, and character are perpetually turning up. But there is a regular art in this study; we must generalise and abstract, and not mistake the accident for the essence. I once heard Mr. Dickens say, that he was constantly receiving letters with humorous suggestions, touches of character, of comedy and the like, which he found to be of no value on this account. We must follow the methods of men of science,

who compare and observe a great number
of specimens until they discover one note.
And thus we arrive at the generic type
which will be recognised by all. Single
special specimens—which may have been
copied accurately—will not be recognised,
being unfamiliar. This system is, of
course, opposed to the cheap and familiar
devices which pass current in the profession.
No doubt, there is a sort of rule of
thumb recipe, which, as the player fancies,
answers very well for the pieces, and for
the audience. According as the character
is *labelled*, so must it be throughout. If
it be comic, tragic, grotesque, or eccentric, so he must make it comic, grotesque,
or tragic to the end, and in every sentence.
His assumption is that a particular char-

acter must reveal itself in every utterance and motion, otherwise it will not
be recognised. The results are, those distortions and exaggerated caricatures of
human nature, to which we are now
grown so accustomed, that we see them
without surprise. We are ever comic
or tragic throughout; every moment
we intermit: it is only when the occasion
arises that the genuine display of native
character is provoked. It is like the
conscientious actor who blacked himself
all over to play Othello.

Acting is popularly supposed by our
journeyman to be a faithful, photogra-
phic imitation of the figures before us in
real life, with all their ways, tones,
peculiarities of speech, gesture, dress, and

the rest. This idea is born of the gross realism so popular in our day—for it is a day of servile copying and imitation, and realism reigns in every art. But acting, in its true sense, is a very different thing. It is an intellectual process, and deals with what is within. It is the art, as we said, of exhibiting *character*, and all the phenomena of character. You cannot *copy* character, but you can reproduce it. Mere servile copying of the outer crust — of the clothes, manners, peculiarities, etc., is not acting; it is merely exhibiting or performing. I will show the difference between the two systems by a familiar illustration. We sometimes see on the Academy walls the portrait of some successful trader, some local functionary, whose vacuous face, composed to a pompous dignity, and saucer-like eyes, excite our mirth or ridicule; yet his friends recognise it as a perfect likeness, and the painter can truly say, " I copied the man faithfully, exactly as I found him : there he is to the life." Yet it is no likeness. Now suppose the sitter to have fallen into the hands of a real artist—a Sir Joshua Reynolds or a Sir Thomas Lawrence, or our own Sir Frederick Leighton—the result would be very different. Such a painter would say to himself, " This must be a success-ful man; for he has fought the battle of life well; he has encountered and tri-umphed over many difficulties, and must have shown sagacity, cleverness, shrewdness in his trade. When he composes himself to a formal attitude of dignity, and strives to look 'genteel,' he will cease to be himself: his mind will be eclipsed, and his face assume a vacuity. But I will pierce to his real and better nature, and show him with his faculties kindled, and stimulated by his favourite calling." And the portrait that is the result will be full of life, shrewdness, and intelligence. There is the difference between acting of character, and the exhibiting merely external accidents.

I venture to say that this principle here illustrated, if duly studied and developed intelligently, would help to make a good actor.

And, curious to say, after all this minute

and laborious copying of the dress-coats and the button-holes, and the cigarettes, the results are usually distortions, and untrue to life. And this, not on account of any ignorance of the manners and customs of society, but from the false emphasis laid on what are mere trivial *accidents*, mistaken for the essence. Here is an example. There are two young men of high fashion in correct evening dress, with pink handkerchiefs protruding from their waistcoats. One is telling the other of his critical position— " I'm in a hole, my dear boy," he will say ; " I· am stone broke;" or that his lady-love has rejected him—he at this critical moment pulls out his cigarette case, and strikes a light. Now, at any crisis or agitation, the last thing one thinks of is pulling

out and lighting a cigarette. They have
seen, no doubt, a couple of youths coming
out of a club, and lighting their cigarettes,
and there seemed to be something gay and
degagé in the process. So they imitate
them. But this was in another situation altogether : it is a moment of relaxation. They
are going into town, or to the Park. But
the actor jumps to the conclusion that the
operation is invariable, and done at *all*
seasons.

Every dramatic or spirited representation
should be a selection, whereas commonplace minds always run into particulars.
They are concrete ; the dramatist is always
abstract ; a painter selects, a photographer
must put in everything, bad and good. The
Robertson school failed in this, because it

was fancied that by reproducing the outward characteristics of society—the flirtations, trifling talk, etc.—they were producing something dramatic. Now, these peculiarities have passed away, and with them the Robertsonian drama itself. But Shakespeare and the great comedy writers dealt with human character, and the points of character that belong to every age and every comedy, and they have lasted. The actors who practise themselves in these trivial surface matters are wasting their powers—they are not acting at all. We have only to reflect that the ordinary conversation of daily life is really irresponsible; half of it, or three-fourths of it, being verbiage and repetition; we often do not heed what we are saying. Often it is mere

trivial nonsense. But what is dramatic
.should be strictly selected and representa-
tive, just as in the case of a very famous
book—Boswell's " Johnson."

Close observation of character has been
the practice of all great actors; not with
the view of imitating peculiarities, but of
obtaining hints or suggestions which they
can develop or apply, even in a different
and unexpected way. In common talk
many delicate and meaning intonations, un-
studied and unprepared, lend effect to what
is said. These inflexions ought to be remembered, M. Dupont-Vernon says, " like
a tune.". Notes of character must be
widened when brought into use, and everything avoided which is special and individual.

Charles Lamb has truly said that the

infirmities of old age, the disagreeable incidents of sickness, and dying scenes, should
not be presented on the stage, or, at least,
insisted upon. In real life these are
mere accidents and disabilities, matters
which disturb the regular course of things,
to be kept out of sight. There is nothing dramatic in these things. The loss
of a leg or an arm in real life is actually
held to be, so far as it goes, a disability,
a hindrance to action and social life. The
blind, the lame, the deaf and dumb, the
spectacle of dying agonies, of sick beds,
wounds, and slaughter have in them nothing dramatic; they must be endured,
and cannot be stayed, because they are
mechanical sufferings. To *say* or describe
that one is sick, dying or dead, blind or

halt, conveys everything at once. We know the full meaning. It is far otherwise with mental sufferings and emotions. These can be varied or averted, or changed, or suppressed, or abolished with an infinite variety. One may vanquish or be vanquished in the struggle. They are therefore followed with a curious interest. A deaf person is sometimes introduced with a view of causing laughter. Thus there may be legitimate entertainment, when the character is an intrusive or fussy one: the ridicule being, as it were, a penalty or chastisement for other defects.

The truth then is, that realism is opposed to dramatic principles. An old property man once declared, when he saw a live elephant introduced upon the stage, that

"he would be ashamed if he could n(
make a better elephant than that." H
was unconsciously uttering an importar
principle of dramatic illusion. For every
thing on the stage must be prepared an
adapted for its peculiarly artificial atmc
sphere, and duly selected and abstracted.

I once saw an admirable instance c
the reduction to the absurd of our moder
realism. In a certain play a Frenc
waiter came on, who played his characte
so naturally, calling out, "*Siphon, m'sieur
petit verre*," etc., and was so generall;
like a Frenchman, that he gained th·
honours of the evening; and next day
in the papers, it was announced that her·
at last was the true, genuine acting—h·
should have an engagement at once

Years after, it was asked what had become of this promising performer; and the
manager laughingly confessed that it was
no actor at all; that he had simply gone
to a *café* in Soho, and selected an intelligent waiter! What a satire on stage
realism! According to this we could come
at last to do altogether without acting at
all: you have only to introduce something from the street or the outside world,
and you have the true unadulterated
article.[1]

[1] Some years ago, a popular actress was seized
with a desire to play a character which a great French
actress had made famous. She played it; it was a
failure, and she wrote her complaints somewhat
peevishly to the papers, an amusingly naïve production.
She urged that she had done her part; she had
tried everything possible to make it a success. She

But our best protection against this
REALISM is its stupidity. The public
soon tires of it. The first time a *hansom
cab was driven* across the stage, what
tumultuous shouts of delight that greeted
it! But the attraction soon palled. And
no wonder. What could have been the
attraction, considering the vast number of
these vehicles that we see daily in the
streets.

had gone to Paris, seen the play a dozen times over,
had studied the "business" of the actress, had gone
to the milliner, and ordered *replicas* of her dresses.
Was it then her fault if the public did not appreciate?
Now, there was something exquisitely comic in all
this. The force of "make-up" could not go farther.
For she left out altogether the main element—the
acting! It was like the poet who said to Charles Lamb,
that "he could write like Shakespeare if he had a
mind." "So you see," said Lamb, "all that was wanting was the mind."

Study of Character.

Is it fanciful to suppose that defects in
.cting are mainly owing to a want of initia-
ive, and to a habit of following established
)recedents? We have copies of copies:
)ld methods and devices are slavishly imi-
ated, and the young actor thinks he can do
1othing better than model himself on a
;raceful predecessor. Mr. Willard intro-
luced the icy, polished, genteel-mannered
/illain, and all the younger players strive to
)e so many Willards. Mr. Beerbohm Tree
ntroduced the diabolical Italian, and has his
'ollowers. We had a certain " Gunnion," a
,enile rustic, in one of Mr. Pinero's pieces,
ind have been afflicted with numbers of the
,ame pattern ever since.

The average actor has few opportunities of mixing with society, though some leading performers have; he is obliged, therefore, to be content with merely the external marks and tokens, such as he can pick up from a distance. His chief resource, then, is the fixed traditions of the stage; or he has to copy some person who has made a success in one of these parts. There are types which are invariably found in almost every modern comedy, such as the lord or lady of fashion, who must be shown as insolent, arrogant, and haughty, and who refuse to give their lovely daughter to a low-born young·man, but who possesses virtue. Unless this haughtiness and arrogance be expressed in language, how are we to *know* that the lord is so vile? Accordingly, his language is quite outrageous. "You are a plebeian, sir," he will say, "a low fellow; a plebeian has no right to exist, or to breathe the same air with me." No doubt, there may be in the peerages persons of this sort, but they never give utterance to these thoughts, or "give themselves away" in this coarse fashion. Rank is always reserved, and *conveys* insolence rather than utters it. It is so with the lady of fashion, who is all wrong as a picture, indulging in screams of stage laughter, walking about and tapping everyone with her fan. And it will be noted that when the fashionable company adjourns to another room, or to the garden, all file out arm in arm.

Study of character is, no doubt, a very difficult one—almost a metaphysical process, and cannot be expected from the average actor. Moreover, the plays he is set to perform offer him few opportunities, being of a thin, cardboarded texture, and based on mere superficial peculiarities. Study of character requires abstraction and selection, because Nature is very indiscriminate, and mixes up bad and good in her compositions. As I said, to get at real types, we must follow the process that scientific men follow—namely, that of examining and comparing a number of specimens, until we discover the true notes of the species; otherwise we are deceived by what are mere accidents. All this can be shown, or illustrated, by an illustration from the sister art of painting. We sometimes see in a shop window a highly-coloured sketch of a soldier, say a private in the Guards; we also encounter him in some picture in the Academy, sitting, it might be, with a nursery-maid in the Park. He is shown with his vivid coat, correct colours, side-arms, and everything. The painter has simply fetched in a private, and made him sit as his model. But is this a *generic* soldier, or the portrait of a particular soldier? Now, in France, there is a painter of soldiers, Detaille by name, who has produced wonderful and brilliant things of this kind. He limns every arm of the service—cavalry, foot, artillery, and the rest; and looking at his figures, we feel, by a sort of instinct, that they represent not the individual, but the type of the soldier. And what was his method? He lived among them, observed their peculiarities, what was common to every individual. He did not draw from a single specimen, but noted certain points which were common to all, though wanting in particular specimens. There is a peculiar gait, a way of wearing their clothes, above all an expression significant of the mind within—a sort of good-natured simplicity which is the result of the profession itself. And thus he arrived at a sort of general type. Peculiarities of an individual specimen cannot be recognised by all, but only such as are found in most specimens—the others are accidents. It is only long, minute observation that will discover for us what points are common to every specimen. This, then, is the method that all our great actors, consciously or unconsciously, follow, and it is the only method.

With characters of a lower degree, with which, as the actor has more opportunities of coming in contact, one would have thought he would be more successful. But here the same failure is found. He studies them from *without* and not from within— is content with the crust or shell, not the kernel. Say there is a costermonger, or some character out of the streets, so often presented in what are called the "slum," or public-house dramas. When the grotesque actor goes to work he gives us the costume, the rabbit-skin cap, the corduroy, the horny voice, the slang, the gait, everything to the life. He will talk of his "barrer," address everyone as "guv'nor." But is this all? Does he think of getting at the real nature of the man? He has not studied "the philosophy of clothes." He has not pierced to the costermonger character or nature. The only way to obtain the knowledge of a class is to generalise, and generalisation is only obtained by comparing a great number of specimens. In short, as Diderot has shown, it is not a costermonger or a Jew that is wanted, but *the* costermonger, and *the* Jew—no chance specimen, but the general type. This is the secret of the success of all the great comedies. The types are general, and the characters essential—of the essence, that is—and therefore acceptable to every generation : while characters, such as are found in the Robertson comedies, made up of local accidents and peculiarities, all on the sur-face— such as tea-drinking and small talk—

become unrecognisable by other genera-
tions.

A fair specimen of this distortion can be
shown in the use made of one favourite
type—the stage servant. In every modern
comedy he is introduced, or rather exhibited—not to help the story forward,
but as a comic figure. On the French stage,
indeed, particularly in Molière's pieces, they
are often important characters in the drama,
just as they are in French real life. But
on our boards they merely perform mechanical functions, bringing in a letter or announ-
cing visits. It is obvious that under such
conditions they are not characters at all,
and are like the indistinct outlines in the
background of a piece of tapestry. They
ought really to come on unobtrusively, like

shadows, and so depart. But no, the manager has to pay a salary, and we must make *characters* of them. They are instructed to work up their business, extract a laugh somehow. The powdered menial, too, is invariably represented as a ridiculous creature, always lisping, or drawling, his head thrown back, his arms carried rigidly. The truth is, the average British servant is a person of extraordinary propriety, and we often admire his absolute reserve and quiet indifference. A genuine master of character, in a single touch, showed the true method. Fag, in the "Rivals," it will be remembered, says something disparaging of Sir Anthony to his master, who rebukes him sharply and goes out. The servant, much disgusted, then complains : "Of all the mean things in the world, this venting your ill-humour on another is the meanest." A little page-boy sharply calls to him to go to his master, on which he turns on him and cuffs and kicks him soundly, calling him "*a kitchen-bred puppy.*" Now, this touch goes to the root of character, and belongs to the servant-character in all ages and countries.

Out of what, then, has our actor evolved this false type? He has worked on that superficial system of observation which I before alluded to. As he passes some great mansion he has seen these lofty creatures looking languidly from the hall window, or haughtily addressing trades-men's boys at the area gate. Here, indeed, are their absurdities best displayed. But he forgets that "Jeames" or "Chawles" is here manifested out of his office ; he is not supporting his character. When he is performing his functions, and in strict relation with his employers, these absurdities vanish. This truth, however, an actor has no opportunity of ascertaining, so he must content himself with what he can see. So with the red - nosed, h - dropping butler. Such he has seen in the service of some pompous trader who has a villa in the country, and such, feeling a sort of contempt for their masters, acquire a sort of familiar and grotesque bearing. Or his model may have been the waiter at a public dinner, or some inferior club.

The " Double Intention."

Now we come to a highly æsthetic, and
most interesting question. What is the
foundation of dramatic *interest?* What
is it that holds our eyes enchained to the
stage? This interest is based, I believe, on
a perpetual *uncertainty* or obscurity, always
exciting and perplexing, as to what the
character of our neighbour really is. We
never know what our neighbour really is.
There is always a veil or mask which we
cannot pierce. We do not know that
what he says, or looks, or does, really
represents what is within. There are
ever the two currents—that of the meaning, and that of the utterance; and

G

we do not know that they correspond. Now, this pleasing perplexity is the foundation of the charm that is found in *social intercourse,* in society, and is the base of all wit, humour, irony, *persiflage,* and such things. Thus a person says something complimentary, but his *tone* conveys the reverse: that is irony, or sarcasm. Another may utter his thoughts solemnly, in a grave tone, and yet the speech may be frivolous—that is burlesque: or *vice versa.* If we all lived in a *palace of truth,* and were forced to speak exactly as we felt, all this social intercourse would vanish: it would become, as was said of history, " like an old almanack." We see this when we meet what are called *matter-of-fact persons,* who, as Charles Lamb says, " make every statement as if upon oath." When they speak, the thing is concluded; there is no doubt, no speculation.

And this leads us on to the great charm and mystery of all acting, the " double intention "—this double current, as it were, of sentiment and its expression, and which is the foundation of all dramatic interest. Suppose we say to some journeyman actor of the day, " Why not try and do two characters at the one time ? " I could imagine the smile of contempt with which this advice would be received. And yet there is nothing fantastical in it—it is really possible ; as Hamlet said, " as easy as lying." There is a fine old comedy, " The Beaux Stratagem," in which a young man, in love with a lady in the country, goes down to her house and is engaged as her footman. It may be conceived what a pleasant *imbroglio* arises out of this. Someone was praising Garrick, who played the young man, in presence of Johnson, saying that he acted the footman admirably. "No, sir," roared Johnson, "he does *not* play the part, for "—and mark this!—"he *does not allow the gentleman to break out through the footman.*" We see at once what a revelation is here. It is a perfect guide to an actor. Here are the two characters—the footman above, the gentleman underneath — both displayed together, the gentleman element betraying itself. I know, when I read it some years ago, I was inclined to cry out, "Eureka!" for it seemed to furnish a key to all the principles of the drama. Our average actor would, as a rule, make the character as footman-like as possible, and take credit for doing so. It is *business.*

This invaluable principle of the " double intention " may be applied in innumerable ways, and the intelligent, versatile actor will find it his most useful instrument for the expression of those delicate emotions which go to make up really fine acting. To give one example. It is easy enough, " plain sailing," to exhibit anger, or enjoyment, or any such simple emotions. But take the state of feeling to be presented to be annoyance under apparent satisfaction. The annoyance must break out through the satisfaction, and struggle with it. Such may be called a state of *ruefulness,* a very delicate, compound emotion, and difficult of expression. There is a French piece, ' in which is shown a *viveur*, wealthy, but good-natured, who is preyed on and pillaged by the lady to whom he is attached, but whose demands on his purse grow every day with an alarming *crescendo*. As each claim was made he conveyed in his face and manner this good-humoured ruefulness : there was surprise, with re-luctance, an attempt at smiling complai-sance ; while there could be seen also a sort of painful sense below, to the effect that " this was really going a little too far." Then there was the fear of offending, and yet an affected haste or eagerness to oblige. Our journeyman could only simply show open annoyance.

Slowness of utterance is connected with

deliberate hatred and dislike. The words seem to be chosen carefully, and the slowness is adopted to make them sink deeply and produce the more deadly annoyance. The utterer takes time, so as to enjoy the full effect. It cannot be loud, for the emotions of hatred enfeeble the voice.

A situation that corresponds with this is where there is apparent satisfaction on the surface, with hostility beneath. The words and form of expression are friendly and complimentary, but the meaning is hostile. Such are the "speaking daggers," sarcasm, *persiflage*, banter, and the like. A compliment that is felt to be untrue, or exaggerated, or undeserved, is but an offensive and cutting form of speech. Then there is the display of *contending* emotions, which no *uttered* words will convey : anger, grief, and the rest. Some evil-doer is unmasked ;—there is, first, rage, then mortification, then hatred, and so on. Or someone is compelled to talk with an indifferent air, while his mistress is engaged with a rival ;— the face would show the constrained indifference, together with strained anxiety and jealousy. Uneasiness, too, how difficult to express palpably; though our actor will undertake it, provided you furnish him with suitable *words* of uneasiness. As when we hear—" The fellow begins to suspect something. But no, I must carry it off, and throw him off the scent !" Yet this could be far more powerfully expressed, and ought to be, by mere looks and bearing.

But it will be said all this is fine in

theory, but how is it to be done? The average actor will protest that he is capable of exhibiting only one emotion at a time, and will contract to exhibit it in the most effective way; or he will produce the various emotions in succession, one after the other. But this will be unmeaning. They must be simultaneous. The process is to be learned only by a serious psychological study, and diligent observation of character. The materials are always at hand ;—in the green-room even, complex emotions are being constantly displayed. He has merely to watch and study and copy. He does not do this, for the simple reason that he firmly believes that he has nothing to do with such things. Acting, as he fancies, is to be studied on the *stage* alone ; there are the regular traditions, and the methods of other actors, and that is enough for him.

Of Comedy.

There is no feeling so unique, so in-spiring, or that puts us in such good-humour with ourselves and with the world, as that of comedy. A good comedy is a sort of present to us for our lives; and everyone finds himself, years afterwards, looking fondly to its scenes, and situations, and char-acters, and with a renewal of the enjoyment. Let us think, what could we do without the two *Teazles*, and their scenes; without *Miss Hardcastle* and *Young Marlow*; *Sir Anthony Absolute* and *Sir Lucius O'Trigger?* There have been many definitions of comedy.

"A picture of manners," said Johnson, which does not help us much. I fancy it is based on some such feeling as this—*the spectacle of the annoyances of life, made light, or alleviated, by patience and good humour.* No one is inclined to accept seriously De la Rochefoucauld's cynical speech, that there is something that gratifies us in the mis- fortunes of our friends; and the man that did so would be a malignant wretch. But there is some truth in it, when we look at it in a "comedy" vein—namely, that certain foibles and follies of our friends deserve *correction,* by way of wholesome chastisement —a little mortification, and what is called "taking down a peg," will do them good. It has been truly said—by Swift, I believe— that the finest piece of wit ever uttered, the best display of humour, never produced such hearty enjoyment and hilarity as the pulling away a chair when a person is about to sit down, and he rolls on the floor. Of course, if the victim be seriously hurt, the business becomes tragic, and amusement ceases; but if he accept it smilingly, and show that he is willing to contribute a little to the entertainment of the company, though with some ruefulness, the feeling is comedy. For we see that here is the spectacle of an *apparent* annoyance, alleviated or lightened.

The general tendency is to assume that everything is more serious than it really is. We meet disagreeable things enough in society—contradictions, mortification, ridicule, annoying characters;—we constantly encounter smaller family trials, which are treated

by the sensible person as trifles that are
not to detain him, and which he almost
ignores. When Tallyrand said, *"pour bien
jouir de la vie il faut glisser sur beaucoup "*—
that is to say, " to enjoy life, we must glide
over many things,"—he was not merely
uttering a wholesome truth, but speaking in
the true spirit of comedy. Take, for instance, the vexations from servants, from
nagging wives, and such incidents of the
domestic life. Anyone who takes these
things seriously, only converts them into
genuine causes of trouble, into bitterness
and even misery; whereas, if they are dealt
with as they ought to be, they will dissolve
away. To the looker-on such things
are a source of entertainment—and this
should be the true view for the person con-

cerned. In how many pieces do we find that much-abused, and much-ridiculed, and unjustly-abused personage, " the mother-in-law," furnishing enjoyment to audiences? A really envenomed encounter between such a woman and her son-in-law, who is entering on a serious conflict with her, the one using every method to dislodge her, the other struggling to keep her place, would give no entertainment, and is almost too painful and unpleasant. It is merely vulgar " squabbling." Real comedy is presented when both contend seriously, but good-humouredly,—the lady affecting to hold the position unwillingly,—say from affection to her daughter-in-law, he waiving his strict right, and baffling her by the most effective, yet still courteous, procedure. We see this every day. Thus, all will admire and sympathise with the prudent, sensible man who, troubled with an impracticable wife, keeps her in hand, as it is called, and is never ruffled or fretted. This he contrives by infusing the spirit of comedy into his relations, gliding over trifling issues, or yielding good-naturedly—while he is firm on important points. The weak man will make a battle-ground of such scenes: like those that occur between Sir Peter Teazle and his wife.

Of course our literal actor, ignorant of the true spirit of comedy, will turn this light and futile skirmishing into a solemn *internecine* conflict. On the other hand, a genuine comedian will contrive to give an air of lightness and unreality to the rather solemn struggle which the writer may have furnished him with. Does the average actor think of any of these things? To him is it not all a sealed book, a language unintelligible? Give me *business*, he will say; or, if he meditate comedy, his notion is that of rattling through the part, with laboriously affected spirits, and restless motions. Yet. to an intelligent performer even these inklings of the principle we have been following, imperfect as they are, would furnish him with quite a new light in the interpretation.

It is not too much to say that all comedy turns on these things; they are the staple of the great comedies; that is, an annoyance proved to be no annoyance at

all, by judicious treatment, and alleviated
by good-humour and good sense. In "She
Stoops to Conquer," *Marlow* is thus chas-
tised for his shyness—corrected, as it were
—but he does not suffer seriously. In
"The Rivals," *Sir Anthony* unreasonably
opposes his son's marriage with a lady that
he liked; and the old man's crankiness
is properly corrected, but not with severity.
In "The School for Scandal," the lady's
bickerings with her husband, and her flirtations with *Joseph*, have the air of serious
events; but they are mere light follies,
corrected by the exposure of the Screen
scene.

The genuine "comedy actor," it is to
be feared, has disappeared, and with him
the delightful gaiety of the stage. We

know what it is to be in company with
what is called "a pleasant person," who
puts everything in an agreeable way, and
handles even serious matters in the same
vein. He is opposed to your literal, matter-
of-fact person, who treats things as if he
were upon oath, and who makes every statement with responsibility. All society is
based upon this airy view of things. The
good comedies were conceived in this spirit,
and must be performed in this spirit; but
nowadays the system is to give point and
emphasis to each utterance, bringing out
their apparent meaning with a business-
like purpose.

How exquisite, too, and how seldom
encountered, is the lightly uttered, careless delivery of something that is specially

offensive—some speech reported, and intended to give pain. This airiness is
supposed to convey the idea of irresponsi-
bility, as though the reporter did not
know the value, or meaning even, of what
he was saying. This makes the suffering
of the victim more exquisite; for if the
tale-bearer were to be consciously deliberate, the other would naturally conclude
that it was malice that prompted the repetition—had invented or exaggerated it.
All these delicate *nuances* set the mind of
the spectator working, keep him in a
flutter, as it were, and constitute real
acting. It was this "literal" system that
so depressed Charles Lamb, when a
monument to the poet Burns was suggested. He made a remark to this ef-

fect, "Would that he were among us now!" Two Scotch gentlemen jumped up and exclaimed, "Nay, mon, but he is dead!"

Latterly, we have even had a strange system of modernising the old comedies, making them practical and literal, and recently the vivacious Charles Wyndham ventured the experiment of giving us what was called "*Sheridan Up to Date*," with *fin de siécle* jokes and illusions. This is bad enough, but the purely literal system had set in so long ago as Elia's time.

With masterly analysis Lamb showed what should be the true interpretation of the character of Joseph. He is generally exhibited as a hypocrite of the "Aminadab Sleek" sort.

"To go down now, he must be a downright revolting villain—no compromise; his first appearance must shock and give horror; his specious plausibilities, which the pleasurable faculties of our fathers welcomed with such hearty greetings, knowing that no harm (dramatic harm even) could come, or was meant to come of them, must inspire a cold and killing aversion. Charles, the real canting person of the scene, must be *loved.*" Such hypocrites were secure of their devotees, who relished, or invited, their sanctimonious utterances. Joseph Surface, however, was different. He moved in a free, irreverent society: he had, therefore, to be plausible, and restrain his imposition. It will be seen what a difference this makes. To Lady Teazle he came as the

lover of a pleasing and sentimental sort, not
as the whining utterer of pious platitudes
at whom any lady of spirit would laugh.
And there was the true comedy conception. Mr. Surface was a gentleman. He
moved in satirical society, where any
Pharisaical display would be ridiculed.
He was a man of culture and tact; and
though a hypocrite, he was a genteel,
clever hypocrite.

Let us now apply this test to the famous
Screen scene, when he is making his
advances to Lady Teazle. Speaking of
her husband's treatment of her, and of
her "conscious innocence," he says, " Ah,
my dear madam, there is the great mistake ! It is this very conscious innocence
that is of the greatest prejudice to you.

What is it makes you negligent of forms, and careless of the world's opinion? Why, the consciousness of your own innocence." And then he adds, "Your character at present is like a person in a plethora— absolutely dying from too much health." Now, this is always gravely urged as a serious argument—hissed craftily into the lady's ear; but it sounds truly absurd. The real interpretation is this : in case it were resented, he could urge that it was merely joking, wit, and gay *persiflage;* but, at the same time, there was the art-ful insinuation wrapped up in the wit, and which he hoped would sink. The lady could not be offended.

So with the case of Sir Peter and his lady. There is something painful and distressing, and not at all to be laughed at, in the wranglings of an old man who is married to a young wife. These do not form a proper subject for comedy. But the world has decreed that such an alliance is a blunder, for which the offender must pay *some* penalty; and, in the case of a cantankerous old fellow, a little plaguing is considered by society to be fair and equitable chastisement. The Teazle episode is quite in this spirit—for Sir Peter, as he tells us himself, was only fifty, and would nowadays be considered a youngish man, or in the prime of life. Even after their disputes he speaks of his lady with affection. Yet our modern actors turn him into a crabbed old man, dresses him up as such, and imparts the

greatest acrimony into their marital disputes; and thus the whole spirit of comedy
disappears. Elia, in a well-known passage,
has expounded this true theory in his own
brilliant way, and has furnished actors with
an invaluable *vade mecum* for interpreting
comedy. Indeed, a skilled critic might
thus expound the science of acting, taking the imperishable "School for Scandal"
for his text.

"Sir Peter Teazle," he says, "must be no
longer the comic idea of a fretful old
bachelor bridegroom—he must be a real
person, capable in law of sustaining an
injury—a person towards whom duties are
to be acknowledged—the genuine *crim.
con.* antagonist of the villainous seducer
Joseph. To realise him more, his suffer-

ings under his unfortunate match must have the downright pungency of life— must (or should) make you, not mirthful, but uncomfortable, just as the same pre- dicament would move you in a neighbour or old friend."

We can readily apply these principles to all exhibitions of testiness, parental anger, and family conflicts, which upon the stage are presumed to excite mirth. We are familiar with the cross-grained father, with his gout and stick, who, like Sir Anthony, is always threatening to dis- inherit his son because he won't marry the heiress. He is shown in a fury, choked with passion; it becomes a sort of internecine battle between father and son; so that at the end, we feel that the

animosity has been too serious, and that
the sire cannot yield without humiliation.
But, according to the true comedy view,
the wrath of the old man should be no
more than a senile wrong-headedness, the
wilful and wayward explosions of a good old
fellow who loves his child. The equities of
the situation are with the young man; it
is expected by the audience that, though
the parent's wilfulness should be baffled,
he is still not to be humiliated: for
according to the " double intention " which
is here vindicated, he has at heart his
son's wishes and interests—which he fancies
can only be gratified in his own way.
And so here again we have "the art
of treating lightly the annoyances of
life."

One of the most exquisitely drawn, most delightful, and most difficult of characters is that of young Marlow in "She Stoops to Conquer." Every light comedian is pleased at being allotted this pleasant, gay, and "rattling" young man of pleasure. To give point to the shyness and awkwardness, the actor must assume the gross manners of a lout; and to give point to the impudence, the rollicking airs of a "fast" young "blood." When he is introduced to Miss Hardcastle, the rule and tradition is that he must be shy to extravagance, and there is the established "business" of drawing away his chair, while the lady pursues him, as it were, with hers, until he is almost driven off the stage. Then being told to offer his arm, he is so confused and overwhelmed that he takes her shawl on his arm and walks away with it! The late Mr. John Forster used often to expatiate with delight on the nature and ingenuity that is displayed in this delightful combination, and which is in no wise to be interpreted after this clumsy fashion. In real life we do not find two different characters, in the one person, exhibited in an *alternative* way. Young Marlow was a gentleman who knew a good deal of the world, and it was impossible that he could acquit himself in so clumsy a fashion to a lady. He might be shy, awkward, confused. Of course the actor will urge that unless his faculties be exhibited as completely "dazed," he must have seen that the barmaid and Miss Hardcastle were the same person. But all that he felt was awe and discomfort, so he could not venture to survey seriously this very superior lady. He tries to acquit himself as a gentleman, but only succeeds in being awkward: but this is different from behaving from an absolute idiot or clown. The character is, in truth, homogeneous throughout, and consistent. It is neither shy nor impudent. An ordinary person who has been reared genteelly and in good society would reverse Marlow's methods. He would be at his ease with ladies, and shy and awkward in the company of barmaids. But, owing to the system of exaggerated emphasis, each situation becomes distorted and unnatural.

In another telling situation in the play there is always exhibited the same false principle. When Marlow and his friend arrive at Hardcastle's house, believing it to be an inn, they are welcomed by the host with the greatest cordiality. This the visitors accept as the vulgar obtrusiveness of the landlord. The situation is exceedingly humorous, but requires delicate treatment, as any undue emphasis must at once lead to discovery. But the modern actor, having got the idea of a sham landlord contrasted with sham guests, must "work it up" to the utmost. Hardcastle thrusts himself into the conversation, so as to perpetually suggest the innkeeper, but in a fashion that is quite inconsistent with his being a gentleman; he must act the landlord to show that he is one : while the guests repel his advances in a way that would at once prove to Hardcastle that they mistake him for a landlord ! When a cup of mulled ale is brought in, in which the supposed landlord wishes to pledge them, Marlow takes a draught : Hardcastle puts out his hand to drink next, but it is passed across him to Hastings, who drinks, and passes it back, still ignoring the landlord. The latter, in a sort of pantomime style, puts out his hand each time to secure the goblet, but is always baffled. These absurdities are owing to the belief of the performers that the audience will not understand unless all is writ large. They forget that if they behave so exactly like guests, the eyes of the landlord would be at once opened; and that if *he* overdo the private gentleman, the guests will find out their mistake. In each case the application of the " double intention " furnishes the true method of interpretation, and supplies the audience with the key. The host should " break through " the innkeeper, and the private gentleman " break through " the mere guest at an inn. According to Goldsmith's conception, neither the host nor the guests forget their courtesy or their natural character: both act like gentlemen—the one like the owner of a private mansion, who is puzzled by the free and easy behaviour of the arrivals; the guests, like guests who were half-amused at the overdone attentions of a host,

I

which would be duly charged for in the
bill.

To show that this is not all speculative,
I will take another illustration from that
most admirable of comedies, "The School
for Scandal," and will venture to instruct
the actor, in explaining to him, by a single
instance, how this spirit of comedy is to
be applied and "imported" into a situation.

Trip, it will be remembered, was Charles
Surface's valet, and when Moses, the Jew
money-lender, comes to the house, Trip
waylays him with proposals for pecuniary
assistance. "And you, Moses, have you
been able to get that little bill dis-
counted?"—"It was not to be done,
indeed, Mr. Trip."—"A small sum—but

twenty pounds. Harkee, Moses, d'ye think
you couldn't get it me by way of annuity,
Moses?"—"Well, but you must insure
your place. But is there nothing you
could deposit?"—"Why, nothing; capital
of my master's wardrobe has dropped
lately. *But I could give you a mortgage on
some of his winter clothes, with equity of
redemption before November, or you shall
have the reversion of the French velvet, or a
post obit on the blue and silver.* These, I
should think, Moses, with a few pair of
point ruffles, *as a collateral security,*" etc.
Witty and lively as this is, it is curious
to think that it rarely produces any effect.
The actor, with the best intentions, and
determined to make the most of his Trip,
will emphasise these money-lending allusions

to the best of his powers and talents. He "brings them out," as it were, with studied point and weight: but the audience listens without a smile, thinking it absurd and out of drawing that a common valet should seriously propose "a mortgage on winter clothes, with equity of redemption before November." But now let us consider for a moment what is the true view. As we know, the money-lenders were preying on Charles Surface: coming in and going out continually. His valet came to know them intimately, and to know their ways. As he waited at table or passed in and out of the room, he caught up the technical phrases, "equity of redemption," "mortgage," "foreclosure," etc. He believed in and reverenced the power

of these things, though he did not understand their meaning very clearly. Everyone that has experience of the servant's
mind knows how delighted they are to use
strange and difficult terms, as if in a
cabalistic sense. Once enquiring about a
lately deceased friend, I was assured by his
sympathising butler that what his master
wanted was " staminer,"—" staminer," he
repeated over and over again, hugely en-
joying the word. Trip, therefore, was not
solemnly engaging to mortgage his master's
clothes: he fancied that something could
be done by the use of these magical terms—
that it raised him to the level of his betters.
Now, if an actor approached the part in
this spirit, with a sort of desire to set
himself on a level with those above him,

and a grave earnestness and faith in the terms he used, we would have the true comedy spirit.

It always seemed extraordinary that those weak, ill-natured creatures, *Sir Benjamin Backbite*, *Lady Sneerwell*, and the others, should have talked so wittily. " Come, come," says *Sir Benjamin*, "'tis not that she paints so ill; but, when she has finished her face, she joins it on so badly to her neck, that she looks like a mended statue, in which the connoisseur may see at once that the head is modern, though the trunk's antique." Every one has felt this, and the scene rarely "tells," because of the studious intention and consciousness with which the wit is delivered. But what is the true key? Why, that the malignancy and venom of malignant people often furnish them with wit—it barbs their tongues. It is difficult to say a really good-natured witty thing, or tell a *good-*natured story that shall have point; but not so difficult to say *ill-*natured things, and even ill-nature can be entertaining.

How delightful, in real conversations, are what are called careless utterances, light criticisms of serious persons and solemn things! The satisfaction, perhaps, arises from the sense that this airy treatment of important matters proves that they are not such serious matters. On the other hand, what a trial is the matter-of-fact personage, who insists on everything being stated, as if " upon affidavit." And how many actors are there who thus solemnly declare their opinions? With them tone and sense must exactly correspond; whereas, in real acting, it is an art to use a tone that shall be opposed to the proper sense. A serious thing may be said lightly or humorously, or *vice versâ*. It is art to sustain a conversation on some trivial or indifferent matter; while something indefinable underneath, either in the tone or in the air, conveys that the player is speaking in another language altogether. This forms the very highest entertainment for the spectator, and the duplicate interest holds him enthralled.

Of Writing Plays.

Great interest is indeed now being taken in the subject of play-writing, and surprise is expressed that writers of wit and genius do not use their talent to supply the theatres with "good pieces." An important question here suggests itself: Which have the most potent influence—actors on plays, or plays on actors? We can have little hesitation in answering that, whereas a good actor will not make a good play, a good play may make good actors. What true dramatists are, and how extraordinary is their effect both on audience and actors we see by the constant recurrence to Shakespeare,

Goldsmith, and Sheridan. Their characters never grow old, and given to an
ordinary actor, actually inspire him : he
cannot help " doing something with them."
These masterpieces are like realities : that
is, the characters seem different at different
times. One actor will take one view,
another a different one. We also hear
a complaint now-a-days that "the literary element " in a play is not . welcomed, though a conscientious author may
strive hard to get it accepted. It could
be easily shown that the " literary element "
is essential to a play, and that anything
without it has no claim to attention.

An interesting question is whether character or story should be the basis of a
play. I venture to think that all true

works, particularly comedies, must be
founded on character. A character is,
in fact, a story, or contains a story.
Conceive the character, and on the instant all the situations, perplexities, and
conflicts, in which the character must be
entangled, necessarily suggest themselves.
On the other hand, when the opposite
course is taken, and we start from a story,
to make a story, there is no spontaneous
development—the thing is complete, and
there is the artificial process of fitting
to it suitable characters. An actor who
has to interpret a story is, as it were,
borné, and confined within strict lines;
but give him a genuine character and it
inspires him. It has all the vitality of
character in real life, which is ever

Protean, and ever novel in the luxuriant shapes it assumes.

A hint of the curious truth, that "character is story," is indicated very clearly in the significance of the titles attached to French pieces, and which are often in themselves a story, or suggestion of a story. Take, for instance, "Le monde ou l'on s'emue," which in itself seems a philosophical epigram : there we see the whole play suggested, the "world," which it is supposed to entertain by its measured wit and cleverness, is instead "bored" by these pretentious, affected figures, instruments of insipidity. A glance at the title calls up these personages. ; Many other pieces of this kind could be named, such as "Les surprises de divorce," "Divorçons," "Le question d'argent," "Le gendre de M. Poirier."

The dramatists of our day are clever men, and, it must be said, are obeying the form and pressure of the time, and still more of the public, in supplying a particular form of article. They furnish plenty of eccentric and amusing types —which "serve," and serve well. But there is little display of the knowledge of character, or of that art of making character pure and simple work out a story. If we contrast Meissonier with the ordinary painter of *genre*, we shall see something of the difference between the old comedy of character and that of our day. The French painter gives a scene—say the "Renseignements"—a peasant giving information to an officer and some soldiers, in a wood. A homely, commonplace incident, but how dramatic—what an air of nature! The reason is that the painter roused his imagination, had seen how the incident must have occurred, and had called up the scene before him. Moreover, he knew the dramatic side of human character, and how people must behave in such a situation; or he had had a glimpse of something analogous in civil life—of a peasant before a magistrate. It is curious to compare with this picture one called "Sauve qui peut"—the flight from Waterloo—where the figures, horses, are arranged on stage principles. It is simply a number of mounted men riding away. Meissonier has shown the same dramatic feeling in the wonderful " 1814," and in all his single figures, where he has found the dramatic *mot*—not by copying from a model in the proper attitude, but by study of character.

It is the fashion now to talk of the " ludicrous failure of Ibsen," while many a critic triumphs in his " I told you so " prognostication. But this seems a short-sighted view. Ibsen may not have proved attractive to the public, for whom he is at present too strong a meat, owing to his repellant " forms," and to the overstrained situations and characters, the local allusions, the coarse, gross topics in which he chooses to wallow, and which have been too much for the average spectator. But for all that, the principles have sunk deeply, and will reappear under more attractive forms.

Our dramatists have been impressed, in spite of themselves, and will reproduce them, after their own fashions; audiences also, in spite of themselves, will unconsciously require Ibsenism in some shape.

Already there is a protest against the old stage *conventions*, as they are called, the manufacture chiefly of the stage manager, and adopted slavishly by the writers. This cry against long established rules and formulas is gaining in strength and volume, and it is actually assumed that these are so many fossilised restraints which fetter the exertions of talent. There is even laughter at the "curtains," the concluding situation "led up to," *secundum artem*, and the "discoveries," methods of "getting off," and the like. This is a mistaken view.

In every art are found these ancient conventions, which even the greatest masters find it profitable to adhere to, and which cannot be departed from without confusion.

Scenic Effect.

The art of scenic effect or of illusion, with its accompaniments of scenery, decoration, and dresses, should be scientific, and founded on regular principles. To produce an appearance of reality, objects have to be made unlike reality, according to fixed rules. This principle is, of course, common to other arts, such as painting and architecture. What is intended to be seen at a distance under artificial lighting, and by large numbers

K

at the same time, must be treated in a particular fashion. But in no department of life are such effects produced in so limited an area, and in so short a space of time, as on the stage. Streets, castles, cities, houses, are constructed in a few minutes, only to disappear and give place to structures as imposing. These changes are wrought by applying a few conventional principles which have really scarcely altered during a period of two centuries —as in the case of the steam-engine, which, in spite of improvements of detail, remains practically the same as in the days of Watt. At the present moment the conventional scenic effects are brought to the highest perfection; and it may be said that, whatever task is set to the

scenic artist, provided he be found resources in money and means, he is certain to carry out.

Up to about thirty years ago, there
was a regular system of scenery, and of
working scenery, in the theatres of the
world, which had been in use for nearly
a couple of centuries. Great theatres,
such as the Scala, San Carlo, Bordeaux—
as we can see from the published plans
—were all fitted up on the same system.
Over the stage was a series of flying
galleries, and along the sides a number
of props or shafts, while in the roof was
an elaborate system of drums or wind-
lasses contrived to secure as much power
as possible. These were connected ingeniously with a vast system of counter-

poises, which ran in grooves down the walls. The moving of great weights in a theatre is contrived on this principle of balances, which ensures an even, equable, and certain motion, the counterpoises raising the machine, or object, and being merely controlled by the workman at his drum. The curtain, the drop-scene, even the vast opera-house chandelier, weighing many tons, are also so nicely balanced that a couple of men can raise or lower them. This power of the counterpoise was largely and ingeniously applied in spectacular plays which were in vogue twenty or thirty years ago, notably at the Gaieté, in Paris, or in our own pantomimes, when the engineers of the stage exhausted themselves in devising trans-

formation scenes which took, perhaps,
twenty minutes to unfold. The basis of
all such displays are large platforms, or
"equipments," as the French call them.
They are the essential portions of every
"transformation," and consist of a large
stage rising slowly from below, and suspended by ropes and counterpoises, and
so nicely balanced that a couple of carpenters can raise them, although burdened
by a score of *figurantes*, each strapped to
her "iron." This is the principle which
underlies all these effects, but it is infinitely varied, and there are even platforms upon platforms which rise in their
turn after the first has been raised.

It is admitted that the English are
foremost in all the mechanical arrange-

ments of the stage. The *trappe anglaise* is an English invention, and is more thought of abroad than it is here. A spirit or a genius will of a sudden disappear through a wall; and this is arranged by the "English trap," which consists of a number of elastic leaves of steel or twigs, like two combs placed with their teeth together. These are covered with painted canvas like any scenic door. The actor flings himself against it; it lets him pass through, then flies back to its original state. The same principle is carried out on the stage itself, when a pantomimist seems to pass through the boards, which close after him. The English trap, to be effectively used, requires a sort of courage and daring, as the effect depends on its being, as it were, recklessly done. The French players, as a rule, do not relish the process. It is this native boldness that ranks the English as the first pantomimists and " tumblers." The same courage is shown by the girls who are engaged in pantomimes, who suffer themselves to be hoisted up on irons some thirty or forty feet.

It may be interesting to consider for a few moments some of these mechanical *tours de force.* The same principle is applied with little variation in all. I will then pass on to the remarkable changes that have recently taken place in the scenic system.

Few devices were more ingenious than

that of appearing to give motion to the stage representing the deck of a ship. This was first attempted at the French Opera, when the opera of "L'Africaine" was re-presented; and when, the word being given to change the course of the vessel, the stage was seen to swerve to the right or left. This was in great part an optical delusion; the back portion of the stage, where the stern was exhibited, was a large platform nicely balanced, which swayed round as required, moving with it the gunwale of the vessel. But the rude, time-honoured fashion still survives, without any change, of producing the motion of the angry billows by a painted cloth, which a number of men or boys, lying on their backs, agitate with their legs. Nay, up to this very year, this venerable but effective practice was pursued at one of our leading theatres.

There is a material peculiar to the stage, and invaluable to the scene-painter, of which profuse use is made at Drury Lane, at pantomime season. It is known as " Profile." Large surfaces of wood, about half an inch thick, are covered with strong canvas, saturated with glue and put away to season. Out of this material is cut all the edgings to scenery, foliage, capitals of pillars, and the like, which formerly used to be cut out of pasteboard and nailed on. In the rough changes attendant on a great pantomime, this solidity is x essential.

Conflagrations on the stage seem alarming things enough, from the thick volumes of smoke, the crimson glow, and masses of flame, and many think the risk is serious; but behind the scenes it seems but a tame process, and is perfectly safe. The effect is produced by burning in a pan a powder called "lycopodium," which gives out clouds of white smoke. On this is cast the glare of the lime light, through crimson glasses, and this gives a red, glowing tint to the fumes, revealed through jagged rents and openings. A huge bellows, like that of a forge, is employed to supply a blast to the fumes; and, to appeal further to the imagination, there are falling beams, fire engines, etc. The important principle here indicated is that of using coloured glasses instead of

coloured fires ; it is becoming a great
element in scenic illusion.

A new agent also is the use of steam,
which is supposed to give the vaporous
effect of clouds in motion, hitherto attempted by "gauzes" and painted cloths.
This was first used at the Munich Opera-
house, and was elaborately applied in the
Lyceum " Faust." A regular steam boiler
or generator is fitted up under the stage ;
at the proper moment a number of cocks
are opened, and the whole scene filled
with vapour. Everyone will recall the
first dramatic appearance of Mephisto-
pheles' face through the clouds. This
shows how every resource is being enlisted
in the service of the stage. Electricity
has also contributed its power, and blue

fires are seen to flash along the blades of Faust and Valentine. The pure electric light, though it has been a good deal displayed in panto-mimes, seems to be rather cold in its effects.

Nothing caused such mystery and as-tonishment as the well-known apparition of the " Corsican Brothers," which ad-vanced slowly, and at the same time kept rising, whilst no opening in the stage was visible. This was contrived by an inclined plane with two ledges or rails, starting from below the stage, and ascending at a gentle slope to the opposite side. A level stand was inserted at the bottom between the ledges, and on this the " Corsican Brother," or his double, took his stand. In the stage was an oval opening sufficient to let a figure pass through, the edges of which were lined with bristles or brushes, and which made the opening, as it were, fit close to the figure. This opening was fixed between two travelling planks or flexible strips duly jointed, on the principle of the wooden shutters which roll up and down in front of shop windows. This strip, for the time appearing to be part of the stage, is wound on the same windlass or drum to which the rope that draws the stand up the inclined plane is attached, so that both the aperture and the stand advance together. By the time the journey is completed, the flexible covering has been wound round the drum. Simple as this appears, much ingenuity is required to make all work smoothly, and a hitch or jamb would be serious.

Formerly a large sheet of iron, hung up at the wing, was rattled noisily to give the effect of thunder, but the modern fashion is more terrible and effective. In the larger theatres the property room is placed over the audience; a sort of truck laden with round shot is wheeled along, which tilts over, and sends the balls tumbling slowly over each other, followed by a hollow, reverberating sound, as they trundle along the floor. For the lightning, a long tin tube with a spirit-lamp is used; a powder is then blown through, which takes fire as it passes by the flame, and gives out a vivid flash. A more effective mode is to cut out of the scene zig-zag strips, in imitation of forked lightning; these are covered with varnished calico, painted, and a light flashed behind. Rain is imitated by the rolling of peas in a long tube; wind, by revolving a roller against a rough cloth. The most absurd attempt at illusion, and which is still retained even at first-rate theatres, is the attempt to represent any crash, such as the breaking open of a door, or the falling downstairs. This is invariably done by an extraordinary sound of springing a large rattle with perhaps a heap of broken glass emptied from a basin. Battles on the stage are common enough, and cannon and muskets are discharged with good effect, a sort of drawing-room cartridge made of phosphorus having been invented specially, which on explosion leaves no trace. In aid of a general engagement there is a substitute in use in country theatres, consisting of a cylinder, studded with knobs, which, as it revolves, strikes against projecting flaps of stiff wood, bending them back and then releasing them, much after the principle of a gigantic rattle. This produces that terrific din as of a volley, and gives a frightful emphasis to the detailed explosions. Great caution, however, has to be observed in the use of fire-arms. The effect of ice breaking up on a vast sea has been successfully portrayed by a curious illusive principle. Strips of whitened canvas representing the ice are slowly drawn away to the right and left, revealing the waters underneath, which in their turn are represented by sheets of perfectly black bombasine, not green or blue as might be expected. The effect produced on the audience was entirely owing to the contrast with the glaring white ice, which caused the waters below to look of an inky hue. The result was founded on ocular illusion, and, therefore, on true scenic principles, and its success was in proportion.

The carpentry or joinery of scenes is scientific, and has principles of its own. Nails are not used, and all joints and corners are secured by wooden pins. Iron nails would soon loosen, and the strain split the wood. Scene-men acquire great deftness in moving or shifting these huge frames, which are often some forty or fifty feet high, balancing them nicely as they lift them, and

L

keeping them perfectly perpendicular as they move them.

I might dwell long on these and other mechanical devices; but the principle varies little in most cases. A more important and interesting matter is the curious change and complete transformation that has taken place in scenery within one generation.

It may be conceived that ingenious men, seeing the old and rather clumsy character of scenery, should have often tried to introduce a more purely scientific system. When the Paris Opera was being built, a crowd of inventors came forward with various schemes. One M. Raymond submitted models of a kind of panoramic structure, which filled the back of the stage in a semi-circular fashion, thus doing away with side scenes. The sky was formed by a hemisphere, so that the whole had the appearance of the apse of a cathedral. On these hemispheres moved, something after the fashion of the cowl of a chimney pot. On this framework the various scenes were painted, and could be moved around as change was required. The difficulties of this scheme were obvious—the least of which was the certainty of catching or "sticking," the impossibility of putting away the semi-circular scene that had been removed, while all the supporting ribs would be certain to imprint blackened marks on the canvas. Moreover, as "borders" were abolished, the problem of lighting would have to be met.

Foucault, the well-known deviser of the pendulum experiment, suggested a semi-circular back scene, with a series of semi-circular side scenes in front, and it was supposed that all these curves would blend into each other, and present an indistinct idea of distance. It was found, however, that it was necessary to be exactly in the centre of the house, otherwise all the converging lines would not meet the eye. In every other part all seemed awry, as it were, and the effect was lost. In short these ideas were found Utopian, and though premiums were offered and every inducement held out to men of science and ingenuity, the result is that the most costly of modern theatres—and it cost four millions sterling—retains the old-fashioned system.

The difficulty of dealing with the floor of the stage, the banks, hills, flights of steps, etc., which are so common in operas, also exercised the inventors. For the new Paris Opera House some ingenious plans were offered, and one was seriously entertained. This was of dividing the whole stage into small platforms, each supported on pistons moving up and down in hydraulic presses. A lever, put in motion by the stage manager, would thus elevate or depress any sections of the stage to the height or depth required. This was ingenious: it was elaborated with care and all but adopted, but the objections were found insuperable. The space below the stage would be lost, being filled up with pumps and apparatus; there were nearly a hundred pistons, but the real danger was the almost certainty of some part of the machinery getting out of order. The system was actually adopted at the new Vaudeville, but never came into use.

In the Madison Square Theatre, New York, there is an odd invention of a double stage, one under the other, which descends and ascends, much like a hotel lift. Thus, when one act is going on, the portion below is being arranged for the next, and when the drop scene falls, the stage ascends and gives place to the next shelf. This apparatus weighs many tons, but the whole is so well balanced by counterpoises, that four men at a windlass can move it. But this *bizarre* idea is more ingenious than practical: as there must be an interval

between the acts to give the audience rest
or repose, it is nearly always quite sufficient for the re-arrangement of the ordinary
stage. Another New York novelty, adopted at two theatres, is the placing the
orchestra over the stage. At the Lyceum,
in that city, the music gallery is suspended in the air, between the drop scene
and the curtain, and when its functions are
over, is drawn up into the clouds. It must
be said that nothing is gained by these
fantastic arrangements, save a sense of
novelty.

Under the old system of flats, side scenes,
and borders, we can all recall how a change
of scene used to be affected. A shrill
whistle was heard, a series of grooves
working on hinges was let down for the

side scenes to run in, one set was drawn away and another pushed forward, whilst the back scene, divided into two portions, met in the centre with a sharp report, or parted. In most foreign theatres, the side scenes work in slits in the floor of the stage, and really travel over the mezzanine floor below on what are called "chariots." Mr. Fechter, when he took an English theatre, introduced this system, as well as the sunken footlights. This arrangement of borders and side scenes is still necessary in large theatres with vast spaces aloft and at the sides, which it is necessary to cover in, and which it would be too costly to do by the enclosing scenery now fashionable. This old system was to be seen in full work at the late Olympic Theatre.

The first change in this system took place some fifteen or twenty years ago, when what was called "built-up-scenery" was introduced. This unhappy innovation, thought to be an improvement, has done much mischief, both to the form of the play and its dramatic interest, as well as to the sense of illusion. Owing to the bulk and ambitious character of these vast structures, it was impossible to change the scene often, hence each scene was an act, or else there was a profuse use of carpenters' scenes. The elocution and utterance of the actor suffered, his voice having to struggle with these huge and impeding constructions. At this period — only a few years back — whole plays were written to exhibit what was

called a sensation scene, such as a representation of Charing Cross or Waterloo
Bridge, with which audiences were
enchanted. A play which depended on
one of these trophies was necessarily poor,
and it may be said plainly that such
things have no connection with dramatic
interest. All this meant the introduction
of that *realism* whose vices we have been
considering. What Lamb has so often
enforced in reference to realistic character
applied equally to scenery. We go to
the theatre, he says, to escape from real
life, not to bring it there with us, and
in this view scenery should be as *general*
as possible. Indeed, it always seems that,
in proportion as the scene appears of
this solid character, it enfeebles the airy

and romantic character of the play. A more serious objection to these elaborately built-up architectural scenes is, that the rules of perspective and distance cannot be properly carried out. A range of realistic pillars, for instance, may be graduated in size and shortened, as they lie farther off, so that the last shall be about two or three feet lower than the first. But such shortening in nature is not so abruptly done, and requires long distances; and on the stage the human figure, which is the scale by which the audience must measure everything, cannot be thus arbitrarily abridged.

The ingenuity of modern scenic artists, in obedience to the wishes of the dramatists who desired a freer hand, and who felt cramped by being allowed only one scene in each act, discovered a mode of changing these heavy sets in sight of the audience. This consisted in "turning them inside out," as it were, while removing them, or in turning the back to the front, or in drawing over one portion to the right, so as to uncover the inner side. There are the gravest objections to this monstrous and cumbrous system. It is, in the first place, a most effective destroyer of illusion and dramatic effect; for after such a grotesque mode of change, with many wheelings, grumblings, and creakings and heavings, the mind is quite perplexed with speculations as to what will be evolved out of such extraordinary gyrations. To see a tower travelling on castors about the stage, and then turning right round, so as to exhibit a portion of the interior of a room, destroys all idea of dramatic propriety. The expense, too, of these gymnastic scenes is immense. Indeed, the extraordinary shifts and contrivances to compass this *changement à vue,* as the French call it, are truly grotesque. Not long since at a leading West End theatre, when a room was to change to a village green, after the tables and chairs had been drawn off in the usual way by cords, the large carpet might seem a difficulty; but it had been attached to the bottom of the ascending ball scene, and ascended with it!

With all these realistic displays the result has been a real loss of illusion.

The light has become so profuse and
glaring that all distance and mystery is
lost, while the scene painters are compelled, in self-defence, to make their
colours as fiery as possible. There is
one theatre, however, where true feeling
and mystery and illusion is carried out
under the most poetical conditions. I
allude, of course, to the Lyceum. Here
we find a most accomplished artist, Mr.
Craven, worthy descendant of the line of
Beverley and Stanfield. The Lyceum system is worth considering for a few
moments, as here is cultivated the sense
of illusion in the most perfect way.

The system in use there, is like most
systems of the day, an eclectic one; it
selects and combines what will best carry

out its purpose. It is a mixture of the old "border" and "flat" systems, and the "built-up" one. *Any* method, in short, that will carry out the end, is adopted. There is a great advantage to start with in the beautiful and well-designed stage, well suited to set off the pictures of the artist, which are most welcome to the eye. But the charm is in the judicious control and subordination of all these agents to the general effect.

There is also another element used here with extraordinary effect, namely, an elaborate system of varied lights, which is brought in aid of the colouring. These are apart from the usual gas "battens"; and are contrived by a complex series of coloured glasses or "mediums" which are changed

and experimented upon till the effect is
found. Mr. Craven once explained some
of his views, and they are interesting. " A
particular art of painting," he said, "has to
be applied, by which seemingly hopeless
combinations are made appear as one
harmonious whole—giving height, breadth,
distance, space, light, and colour; the
effects of day, night, wind, and rain; the
general hurly-burly of the tempest, and the
calm of the mid-day sun." In the scenes
for "Romeo and Juliet," at the Lyceum,
and afterwards in " The Mikado," he
succeeded in portraying a bright, clear,
blue sky by the introduction of an entirely
new colour; the result was abundance of
light, air, and colour. This subordination
of detail to the general effect is carried out

in every direction. The lighting is subdued so as not to reveal details, the changes
of scene are effected in obscurity ; the
painting and colours are in low, rich tones,
so as to throw out the figures. Every one
will recall the original and strikingly effective use of the "gauzes" for supernatural
effects in "Faust." Another element at
this house is the abundant use of modelled
architectural pieces, such as statues, sculp-
tured pillars, the door of the monumental
cathedral in "Faust," and the elaborate
temple that was exhibited in Tennyson's
"Cup," the pillars of which were adorned
with classical figures in high relief. All
which prodigies, I may say, were wrought
in pasteboard; that is, the design was
moulded in plaster, and sheets of paper

✗ were pasted over it until the desired
thickness was reached. Thus was ingeniously secured all the effect of stone—in
a material excessively light and portable,
and enduring any amount of what is called
" knocking about." Beautiful and satisfactory as these results are; they are not
without drawbacks. This elaborate model-
✗ ling affects the painted portions by contrast, and imparts a flatness to painted
details. An opening scene at the Savoy
Theatre (also Mr. Craven's) represents in
the most perfect way "the last word" of
scenery. Here we have sky borders, and
building up, and coloured lights, and
modelled portions, all with the most
brilliant and satisfactory result. It requires, however, extraordinary efforts to

unite these systems, which are really irreconcilable, as anyone can see, who in a drawing-room scene will note " borders" used as a ceiling in combination with side walls; for the edges of both cross each other at a right angle.

A clever Frenchman, the other day, when shown some triumph of scenery, exclaimed, *Voilà le dernier mot!* He was promptly assured by the manager that, " in scenery there is never the last word— but only the last but one." That is, the scene painter engages, as it is called, " to beat any previous record." But this is surely an unsatisfactory state of things for the public—who will gaze, with but sated eyes, at some spectacle that has cost an enormous quantity of time, thought, and money to prepare. As I said, there should surely be something scientific in this great art of the scene—some principles which should fix the proper laws of scenic effect and illustration. And I propose, before concluding, to formulate a few of these principles.

The first point would be to settle clearly what is the true relation of the spectators to the action on the stage. The popular notion is that they are in the position of Asmodeus; the side of the house being, as it were, removed for their benefit; through the great arch they see a room, a street, a castle. But this is not consistent with the dramatic theory, which assumes that the audience, though at a distance, is privy to all that goes on. The foundation of every drama is, that the audience and author are in each other's confidence; for when the author attempts a surprise on the audience, it is always resented. The situation of the latter is, therefore, that of a person *on the stage*—and the fourth side of the room is really behind the audience. Supposing this view to be well-founded, the peep-show idea of the scene— that is, of the audience looking into another world through an arched opening—will not hold.

The question, " What is the scene ? " and the answer to it, contains the true theory. By existing custom it seems to be held that "the scene" should be a *complete* representation of the locality. If it be a room, it is a complete room; if a square

in a city, it must be an entire square; if
the outside of a house or castle, it must be
nearly a whole castle. Yet in real life,
when some critical incident occurs in, say,
a drawing-room, or in the open street, the
spectator, absorbed in the interest of his
business, takes in, not the entire superficies
of the room, but only the immediate background or surroundings of the incident,
"the zone," as it were, comprising a few
feet around the personages. This is sufficient, and the dramatic absorption allows
of no more. There is an admirable
passage in Lamb's Essays, where he is
criticising one of Martin's great pictures,
filled with architectural details and innumerable figures, and where he sets out
the true principle. "Not all that is

optically possible to be seen," he says, "is to be shown in every picture. In a day of horrors such as Martin's 'Belshazzar's Feast,' the eye should see, as the actual eye of an agent or patient in the immediate scene would see, only in masses and indistinctness, only what the eye might be supposed to see in the doing or suffering of some portentous action." Not all that *is* *optically possible* is to be shown in a picture or a scene! Most expressive words these.

It will be asked, how is this theory to be applied in practice? The answer is that it *has* been applied, and that the old system of flats and side scenes was in a rude way based upon it. A room, for instance, was there: but only so much of the room as was concerned with the action, and this the whole system helped to indicate in the best manner. In the fashion, as it is called, of "coming on" or "coming off," the scene must illustrate, under the modern system, every step of an actor's progress. All that is "optically possible" must be accounted for; he must walk to the wing, open the door, pass through, and close it, disappear. But by the old system the player went off or came on the scene—that is, he passed, as it were, from the zone of action, and merely disappeared at the wing. In real life it would be the same. Were we looking on at a dramatic crisis we would take no note of door, or passage to the door; all that would come within our ken would be that the person had left

the scene of action; the rest is too minute
for observations. All this helps to make
scenery general.

In our modern system this attempting
to exhibit all that is "optically possible,"
especially in built-up structures, leads to
very absurd results. While the area is
constant and invariable, there must be
a perpetual alteration of scale in successive
scenes. The same space serves in one
for the interior of the cabin, in the next
for the interior of a palace, or the elevation
of a built-up castle, or for a large square
or market-place. This is the result of
minute imitation or reproduction of outside
objects. To be at all faithful, it would
require elasticity of space. But in the
old system—*viz.*, the dealing scenically with

the space only immediately round the performers, we have a factor that is always constant, and a scale that does not change. At the same time, the scenic artist who confines himself to canvas, has boundless resources for his perspectives and distant prospects on "the flat," and there is no danger of the scale being disturbed by the figure of the actor.

I can fancy, however, that in time we may revert to this wholesome system, where the relief and distances will entirely depend on the skill of the painter. It is indeed possible, as a painter knows, to make a distinct art of the simulation of raised surfaces. Foreign artists make this imitation of relief and distance quite a study, and in Italian churches we see figures in relief so high as to deceive the eye. At the same time it would be impossible to revert to the old baldness of flats and side scenes without due modernisation. The glare of light in which our stages are bathed is fatal to all illusion— it reveals everything, the rifts in the boards, the texture and creases in the canvas, the streaks of the paint. The light, playing on the edges of the side scenes, would show us that they were mere screens; but with subdued lighting, and low, rich tones and colours, the edges would be softened away, and all made into one whole.

This idea, that the scenic decoration should be bounded by the zone of dramatic interest, is curiously supported by the old

method of lighting. I have mentioned
that in Garrick's time the stage was lit
by no more than four chandeliers, with
a half-dozen candles in each, hung over
the heads of the actors, besides a few lamps
and candles at the wings; thus the light
was thrown mostly on to the faces of the
central figures, and the largest part of the
stage must have been in obscurity. By
this system of a dark background the figures must have stood out with surprising
brilliancy; the eyes of the audience must
therefore have been directed to the illumin-
ated portion, instead of, as now, being
disturbed by the universal effulgence.
We are so accustomed to the light being
cast upward that we now cannot conceive
them in any other position; yet the light

being thrown downwards, as in real life, the unimportant ·legs being left in comparative shade, the effect must have been far better. M. Garnier, the architect of the new Paris Opera House, pleads for the footlights, and thinks it adds an air of youth. The relief of light and shadow makes up half the pictorial effect of life. We can see from the old theatrical paintings in the Garrick Club that the apartments and scenes in which the player moved were lit, as in ordinary life, with visible lamps. But now, with battens and footlights, each with two or three hundred jets all in one blaze, the figures seem part of a glittering tissue, and do not stand out. It does, therefore, seem that these splendid displays rather impair than increase illusion.

Formerly, every one was virtually in the house, the pit (as in the old Haymarket) in the centre, encircled by the boxes. Now, the exigencies of making the house hold as many as possible, have driven the pit into an excavation under the boxes, with the stalls in front. The balcony projects far over their heads. To let the pit have some sort of view, the stalls are sunk down very low. These changes, however justifiable, have affected the sense of illusion in a very remarkable way. To the tenant of the stalls, there can be nothing illusive in what he sees. The same distortion arises from the arrangement of the boxes and balconies, which, in spite of ingenious bends and curves, never supply a suitable or comfortable angle of observation. Now, in the great architectural theatres, such as the noble one at Bordeaux, these matters are carefully looked into. The stalls are placed slightly below the stage, but ascend to the back, while the first tier of boxes is almost on a level with the stage. At the Alexandra Theatre, at Liverpool, the same arrangement is followed, with great nobility of effect. Such is the true disposition of a theatre, and it necessarily excludes the burrowing under the boxes to find space for a pit. The actors' voices are lost in these cavernous recesses; they lose the inspiring sense of having the whole audience before them—the rows of intelligent and sympathetic faces.

Illusion, then, is the great point, and

very small resources will compass illusion. Even the familiar curtain can be made to contribute. It is becoming the fashion to have divided curtains, that fall between the acts, made of real or simulated tapestry. These close imperfectly, and nearly always indicate the "super" behind, who has to rush to hold them together. But does this suggest the idea of the great barrier that should always exist between the mystic scene and the hard practice of life? It imparts a sort of trivial drawing-room association. We feel almost that we might step up on the stage and peep in. But it is otherwise with the old traditional heavy green curtain, which floats downwards with slow and solemn folds. Both curtain and drop-scene represent the barrier between the real and the ideal world. The floating green curtain, on which the eyes of the audience rest during the interval before the performance, has a special significance and a dramatic meaning.

Again, the drop - scene, which marks merely a suspension of the dramatic interest, should not have the solemn finality of the green curtain. It is a subject of speculation what should be portrayed on its simple surface. Sometimes we have seen landscape, by Telbin or Beverley, enclosed in a border, or it may be a grouping of painted draperies and curtains. Garnier, the architect of the Paris Opera House, holds that this is the most fitting treatment, as it represents the function of

N

the canvas, which is to be a curtain—and if these draperies be skilfully executed with pleasing colours, the effect is good. An objection to the landscape is that it impairs illusion, as it is in fact only another scene; and when it rises, some of the effect of surprise is lost when the regular scene appears. This may seem a trivial point, but by being attended to, it fosters illusion.

Space does not allow me to say more, but I think I have indicated, though in a sketchy way, all the crucial points of this most interesting question.

It will be seen that the same principles regulate stage illusion and scenic effects, as those that direct the performance of an actor. The whole is, in fact, homogeneous, and forms one science.

THE END.

WORKS ON THE STAGE.
BY THE SAME AUTHOR.

THE ART OF THE STAGE: Lamb's Dramatic
Essays, with a Commentary.

PRINCIPLES OF COMEDY AND DRAMATIC
EFFECT.

THE LIFE OF GARRICK.

LIVES OF THE KEMBLES.

THE ROMANCE OF THE ENGLISH STAGE.